CHILDREN AND ARSON
America's Middle Class Nightmare

CHILDREN AND ARSON
America's Middle Class Nightmare

Wayne S. Wooden

and

Martha Lou Berkey

PLENUM PRESS • NEW YORK AND LONDON

Library of Congress Cataloging in Publication Data

Wooden, Wayne S.
  Children and arson.

  Bibliography: p.
  Includes index.
  1. Arson—United States—Psychological aspects—Case studies. 2. Juvenile
delinquents—United States—Attitudes—Case studies. 3. Adolescent psychol-
ogy—United States—Case studies. 4. Criminal psychology—Case studies. I.
Berkey, Martha Lou. II. Title.
HV6638.5.U6W66   1984   364.1'64   84-11731
ISBN 0-306-41773-1

© 1984 Wayne S. Wooden and Martha Lou Berkey
Plenum Press is a Division of
Plenum Publishing Corporation
233 Spring Street, New York, N.Y. 10013

Printed in the United States of America

I hear the alarm at dead of night,
I hear the bells—shouts!
I pass the crowd—I run!
The sight of flames maddens me with pleasure.

Walt Whitman, *Poems of Joy*, 1860

ACKNOWLEDGMENTS

The authors would like to take this opportunity to thank the many individuals who contributed to this book.

A special appreciation goes to Paul Boccumini, Director of Clinical Services for the San Bernardino County Probation Department, and the Probation Department's staff, including Barbara Ward-lawe and Stan Brown. We wish to thank Keith Griffiths, Norman Skonovd, Roy Lewis, Carl Jesness, and James Turner of the research division of the California Youth Authority. Joseph D. Piscioneri was also most helpful in this project. A particular thanks to Kevin Bolinger for his assistance with the statistical analysis of the study. We are equally indebted to Peter M. Nardi and Gary A. Cretser for their editorial comments on earlier drafts of the manuscript.

Others we wish to acknowledge include Kenneth R. Fineman, John Barracato, Dewey Willis, Charlotte Rhea, Saul Niedorf, Dudley Sams, Tom Hopkinson, L. H. Jacobson, Doug McClure, Cal Terhune, Susan Wolfe, John C. Lee, and Jan Gratton.

We also appreciate the special consideration given to us by the School of Arts and the Department of Behavioral Sciences of California State Polytechnic University, Pomona, in providing us with release time and supplies to complete the project.

Finally, we wish to express our deep appreciation to Linda Greenspan Regan, our editor at Plenum. She has offered invaluable help in putting this volume together.

We would also like to acknowledge our production editor, James Knierim, for his work in the production stages of this book.

On a sad note, Martha Lou Berkey succumbed to cancer during the completion of this project. She leaves behind a husband and two daughters. Her special warmth and understanding will be missed. This book stands in her memory as she cared about and helped these young firesetters.

WAYNE S. WOODEN

CONTENTS

Chapter One

INTRODUCTION TO THE PROBLEM

A 10-year-old boy who said he was angry at being spanked by his mother has admitted starting a fire at an apartment building that caused an estimated $85,000 in damages, police said.

A 3-year-old sister was left in one burning bedroom when the boy and a 7-year-old sister ran from the home after the blaze erupted, police Detective James Pearson said. The children were found after midnight four miles from home. The children's father rescued the 3-year-old.

The boy told police he used a cigarette lighter and paper to start the fire in two bedrooms and the living room of his family's apartment, Detective Pearson said. "Kids get mad at their parents all the time but don't usually do something this drastic."

The boy was being held in Orange County Juvenile Hall in Southern California for investigation of arson.[1]

News items like the above, under the headline, "Orange County Boy Says Spanking Drove Him to Start Fire," have become such a common occurrence that they no longer warrant front-page coverage. Relegated to the second section of the newspaper, this "revengeful" boy's firesetting incident was reported alongside two other arson-style fires ignited that same afternoon. In one case a seventeen-year-old male was apprehended for allegedly setting a brushfire that required fifty people to be evacuated and that threatened 100 homes. In another incident, Los Angeles police

1

arrested the teenage sister of a man whom they say burned
to death after he was doused with gasoline in an apartment
fire. In this fire, several residents were injured, including
a pregnant woman who later complained of abdominal
injuries after she jumped from an upper window to escape
the flames.

Nearly everyday occurrences? Unfortunately, yes, if
we look at the figures. Firesetting in America is reaching
what many public officials consider epidemic proportions.
And alarmingly, as our book will show, more and more
of these fires are being set by our nation's youth. And like
the ten-year-old boy who set a fire because of a spanking,
these young arsonists are setting fires for reasons that
seem at first glance to defy comprehension.

It is the purpose of this book to focus on this critical
problem of firesetting by the young. In the chapters to
follow, we attempt to understand the reasons for juvenile
firesetting. We distinguish between the behavioral *characteristics* of firesetters, the several *types* of firesetters, and
the *motives* of firesetters. Further, we discuss the several
distinctive patterns of juvenile firesetters, and we highlight several new fire safety and treatment programs that
are attempting to rehabilitate the firesetter as well as to
educate the general public about the severity of the problem. More to the point, it is the goal of this project to
explore the role that juveniles under the age of eighteen
are playing in this increasing national problem of arson.
America, it seems, *is* burning, and America's children, in
many instances, *are* igniting the torches.

This book focuses on the psychological reasons why
young people set fires, gleaned from a great many original
data. We particularly concentrate in our study on 104
young arsonists who were apprehended during a four-
year period beginning in mid-1979 in San Bernardino
County of Southern California. Added to this analysis is

a discussion of studies we conducted on a comparative group of nonfiresetters; on 536 juveniles who were apprehended for setting fires on school property during a seven-year period; and on 128 fire fighters of one fire department that recently began a fire safety program to help rehabilitate juvenile firesetters. Besides these original studies, we also present several interviews with the public officials who investigate these arson cases, as well as with those who rehabilitate the young arsonists once they have been apprehended.

We will view these juveniles and their firesetting behavior within four general types. First, we discuss the youngster whose curiosity about fire often leads to an accidental fire. We identify this type as a *playing-with-matches firesetter* who is merely engaging in "fire play" rather than in deliberately setting fires. The second type is those troubled youngsters who engage in firesetting as a gesture of displeasure with an often chaotic and disruptive home environment. This type of youngster is identified as our *crying-for-help firesetter*. Our third group is made up of the older adolescent and the teenager who engage in arson as a form of juvenile delinquency. But as we will show, the *delinquent firesetter* differs from other delinquents in critical ways. Finally, the pathological youngster who sets fires with great frequency and ritual is our fourth type, the *severely disturbed firesetter*.

Further, our analysis points out several disruptive patterns and characteristics in the background of young firesetters. The major problem shared by these youngsters is that they come from severely disturbed family environments. Rarely did we find one from a healthy, intact family. And even when the father was present, significant problems existed between the parents or between the father and his children. A second alarming pattern is that many of these young people have been victims of sexual abuse. Although this was more typically true in the case of the few female firesetters in our group, there were several instances where young males had been the targets of sexual assault as well.

A third characteristic common to our firesetters is their poor performance in school. Although often intelligent, these youngsters were frequently truant from school and were disruptive and hyperactive when in school. To take out their frustrations, these youngsters often torched school property, as our analysis shows.

A fourth important pattern illustrates the poor relationships that these youngsters have with their peers. Inadequate in their social skills, our firesetters are often unable to form close friendships. Their lack of assertiveness makes them vulnerable to peer-group manipulation. As we will show, in those fires set by groups of kids, the social misfit in the group was the one who was most encouraged to set the fires. This he or she did as a means of winning the group's approval.

A fifth major distinguishing characteristic is the multiple problems of these firesetters. In fact, we identify thirty-three behavioral characteristics that distinguish the firesetters from the nonfiresetters. Further, according to these youngsters' own parents, the firesetters have had a history of severe behavioral problems. The "typical" adolescent firesetter, it appears, follows a sequence of first feeling isolated, then wandering around, beginning to steal, disobeying and withdrawing from parents and teachers, and finally setting fires. In this continuum, firesetting can be viewed as one form of serious delinquency. These youngsters wait until they are literally "burned out," and then they light something.

Such background problems and characteristics are not unique to firesetters, but what our study shows is that juvenile firesetting *is* an act that differs from other delinquency patterns. Unlike the more frequent juvenile crimes, such as burglary, theft, and rape (crimes that are disproportionately committed by lower-income non-Caucasian males), juvenile arson—a comparatively infrequent crime—is, nevertheless, disproportionately committed by middle-income Caucasian males.

Another surprising finding is the results of the study we conducted on the fire fighters of one metropolitan fire department, which showed that 55 percent of them had, themselves, set trouble fires as youngsters. Furthermore, 9 percent of these fire fighters' children had set fires against their parents' wishes. We interpret these patterns and discuss such issues as why these fire fighters think children set fires, and what role fire departments should play in educating the public about fire safety.

Not only is arson the fastest-growing crime in the nation, it is also the most costly. In addition to the obvious monetary costs, such as medical expenses, lost tax revenue, and police and fire department operations, destructive fires inflict untold misery on families experiencing the loss of lives of their loved ones, including fire personnel. Likewise, no monetary value can be established for the psychological and physical trauma of the burn victim, whose pain is excruciating and whose survival often means living with scars and grotesque disfigurement. Furthermore, not only do forest fires devastate the land with loss of forest and wildlife, but such fires leave the land vulnerable to the seasonal rains, which in turn bring mud slides and erosion. Fire can truly be a deadly and devastating force.

Just how deadly? In terms of actual numbers, according to government figures, 6,020 civilians and 117 fire fighters died in fires in 1981 in the United States. And approximately 300,000 civilians plus 100,000 fire fighters were seriously injured. The total loss in property alone came to $6.4 billion.[2]

But of these fires, how many are actually attributed to arson in that they are deliberately caused? According to 1981 figures, the *Uniform Crime Report*—which bases its data on reports from participating law-enforcement agencies representing 86 percent of the country's population—catalogs 122,610 arson offenses. Furthermore, younger people, under the age of eighteen, accounted for over one-third (38 percent) of the arson clearances (actual arrest *and* conviction) nationwide in 1981. This percentage of juvenile involvement in arson was *higher* than for any other index crime.[3]

According to these government figures, the estimated number of arrests for arson in 1981 totaled 20,600, a 4 percent increase over 1980 and up 13 percent over the 1977 figure. Of all the people arrested for arson, 42 percent were under eighteen years of age, and 67 percent were under twenty-five. Males comprised 89 percent of all arson arrestees. By racial background, 78 percent of the persons arrested nationally for arson were Caucasian, 10 percent were black, 7 percent were Hispanic, and the remaining 5 percent were from other racial and ethnic backgrounds.

With over two-fifths of the nation's arson cases being committed by juveniles, and with arson on the rise, it is hoped that this book will be of interest to concerned citizens, fire-fighting personnel, probation and social workers, the academic community, parents, and elected public officials. Only with a combined and continued effort will we begin to address this growing national concern, and to extinguish these "flames" of youth.

Chapter Two

THE BURNING OF AMERICA

According to the 1980 Federal Bureau of Investigation statistics, the United States has the highest rate of arson in the world. Arson now appears to be the nation's fastest-growing crime, quadrupling during the decade of the 1970s and increasing tenfold in dollar losses during that same time period.[1]

As bad as the arson problem now is, some experts, including the chief arson investigator of the National Fire Protection Association, feel that it may get worse. Commenting on the frustration that many people feel with their public officials, this investigator stated, "Fire setting is a way of lashing out resentment for the environment in which people find themselves. They feel that the government is not concerned, their local government is not concerned, and they say, 'To hell with them—I'm going to burn something.'"[2]

Several factors are at work that inhibit efforts to curb the crime of arson. The primary factor is that arson is often treated as a low priority by law enforcement agencies, fire control agencies, and even the public. Further, there are many distinct and unrelated firesetting behaviors that make it a difficult problem to respond to. Each act of arson may demand a very different response from government officials, the community, and public protection agencies. Finally, arson control programs have been hampered by an inadequate understanding of the scope and prevalence of this crime.

Because of the complexity of the problem, the Law Enforcement Assistance Administration (commonly referred to as LEAA) set forth an "arson taxonomy" that differentiates eleven types or motives for arson in five comprehensive categories. Defining arson as "the willful and malicious burning of property," the LEAA found, for example, that in 1979, 42 percent of the nation's arson fires were acts of (youthful) *vandalism*; 23 percent were set by individuals whose primary motive was one of *revenge* or *spite*; 15 percent were *arson-for-profit* fires, such as igniting businesses to collect on the insurance claims; 13 percent were acts of *pyromania*, set by those who have an uncontrollable urge to set fires; and 7 percent were set by those who use fire as a means of *crime concealment*.[3] Distinctions between these categories are more fully developed later in our study.

In its manual, the Aetna Life & Casualty Company provides its arson investigators with examples of firesetters who fit several of these categories. For example, fires for revenge, according to the manual, are committed by such types as jilted lovers, feuding neighbors, disgruntled employees, quarreling spouses, and people motivated by racial or religious hostility. Citing statistics collected by the company itself, Aetna noted that 47 percent of convicted adult arsonists had committed arson for purposes of revenge, and that 51 percent of fires in churches were of suspicious origin, leading the investigators to claim that these fires appeared to be related to the motive of religious and/or racial hostility.[4]

In citing examples of fires caused by *vandalism*, the Aetna investigators noted that these fires are set primarily by juveniles who are protesting authority or attempting to relieve boredom. Vacant buildings and schools (as we document in later chapters) top the list of those places set on fire for this reason, or rather the latter nonreason. According to Aetna's findings, 75 percent of fires in schools, including colleges, are suspicious in nature.[5]

In general, two types of fires can be distinguished: those motivated by some sort of psychological gain, and those motivated by economic gain. It is the first type that is the focus of this present study, as fires set for economic gain are set primarily by adults. We should emphasize, nevertheless, that, according to criminal justice officials, many of these adult professional "torchers" had a history of firesetting behavior as juveniles.

For the purposes of our study, we use the terms *firesetters* and *arsonists* somewhat interchangeably when referring to youngsters who have been involved with fire play. Actually, *arson* is a legal term, whereas *firesetting* denotes the actual behavior of setting fires in inappropriate circumstances, irrespective of legal status.

Because of the extensive increase in arson in the past several years, Congress in October 1978 directed the FBI to reclassify arson from a Part II to a Part I offense—or higher-priority crime—in its *Uniform Crime Report*. With this action, Congress created a new federal program to combat arson, which charged the U.S. Fire Administration to develop arson detection techniques; to provide arson training and instructional materials; to standardize the collection of arson statistics; and to develop handbooks to assist federal, state, and local officials in arson prevention and detection.[6]

The questionnaire that we used in analyzing and categorizing the four levels of firesetters in our study was taken from the handbook that was developed in 1979 as part of this Congressional mandate.[7] In this regard, our study is the first systematic testing of the items included in the handbook. It serves to show the differences between firesetters and nonfiresetters in terms of their behavior, and to distinguish between the ages and the types of firesetters, the heart of what the *Uniform Crime Report* ordered.

Further, in 1981, despite federal cutbacks in many arson programs for economic reasons, Congress was so concerned about this rising tide of arson that it passed an additional bill requiring local police departments to keep statistics on arson and to report them directly to the FBI.

Changes have also been recently enacted at both the state and the local levels. Since 1980, arson in the State of California, for instance, is a violation of Penal Code Section 451. The potential punishment is now based on the degree of bodily harm or physical injury resulting from the fire, as opposed to the former method of basing punishment on the type and extent of property burned. These changes have been enacted in other states as well.

Penalties for arson can vary anywhere from two to four or six years in state prison for a structure or forest-land fire; to a sentence up to nine years for a fire in an "inhabited" structure that results in "great bodily injury" to either the inhabitants or fire-fighting personnel. On the lesser end of this hierarchical classification system is "arson of property," which carries criminal penalties in California of from sixteen months to three years for fires such as grass and brushfires that do not involve buildings. Penalties for arson in other parts of the country generally follow a similar pattern.

Before plunging into our study, we need to ask some basic questions: What draws these youngsters to fire? Why has fire always attracted people? How has fire been viewed over the ages? In general, what have been some of the historical perspectives on fire?

To begin with, fire has been an element essential to the survival of humankind—not only for warmth, but for protection from predators, as well as for cooking and preserving food. People have been continuously fascinated and mystified by this force of nature. Perhaps this attitude is no better expressed than in the critically acclaimed 1982 film *The Quest For Fire*, in which a band of primitive people search for the means to obtain fire once their precious source has been extinguished. The control and cultivation of fire were necessary for the emergence of modern civilization.

Fire, with its primitive appeal, still carries an innate fascination for most people. The coloring and flickering of flames provide a visual stimulus that serves as entertainment and a form of relaxation for the beholder. Its crackling sound appeals to the ear. The word itself evokes a number of emotional and symbolic meanings. For instance, fire is used symbolically in language to express deep emotional feelings of passion as in "burning with desire" or "flames of passion"; utterances of rage, anger, and torment, as in "a fiery look"; and feelings of being overwhelmed or consumed, as in "you set me on fire" or "you burn me up."

Fire as a feared and respected symbol and element has throughout history been merged with mythological beliefs, religious rituals, and philosophical thoughts. Almost all Greek legends regarded fire as a gift of the gods, or as being stolen from the gods. In the Greek myth of Prometheus, Zeus, in an act of revenge, has Prometheus chained naked to a pillar for having stolen fire from Olympus and for having taught humans how to use it. Fire apparently symbolizes in such legends the human desire for power, destruction, and creativity.[8]

For centuries, fire was considered one of the four basic elements, along with air, water, and earth. Biblically, fire has also been associated with the Diety when, as discussed in the Book of Exodus, Moses is approached by the angel of the Lord in a flame of fire from a burning bush. References to both the punitive and redemptive natures of fire are manifold in both the Old and the New Testaments. The Israelites, for example, were warned in the Book of Deuteronomy that "the Lord thy God is a consuming fire, even a jealous God." In the Book of Mark, hell is described as comprising a fire that can never be quenched.[9]

During the Middle Ages, fire was used literally and symbolically to punish heretics, as burning them at the stake was thought to be akin to their fiery punishment to come in the afterlife. The consequences of this belief were great, and some 200,000 burnings at the stake took place for such crimes as heresy, witchcraft, and sorcery during the Middle Ages.[10]

In primitive societies, fire is often used in purification ceremonies, with persons being required to walk, leap through, or jump over fire. Many societies practiced the burning of live sacrificial victims to placate the gods. An ancient Hindu custom involved the placing of widows on the funeral pyres of their deceased husbands so as to provide the men with their wives in the afterlife.[11]

Fire has long been used in warfare and as a representation of anger. In more modern times, the Ku Klux Klan adopted the symbol of the burning cross to mark the properties of those people whom they wished to intimidate. An effective weapon during World War II was the flamethrower.[12] During the Vietnam war, napalm was a common instrument of destruction.

Arson itself is as old as civilization, but it was not until the nineteenth century that there appeared to be much concern about the motivations for it or about the psychological stability of arsonists. One of the earliest reports was by a medical practitioner in 1837 who wrote of a young female patient who, sexually aroused and "overheated" from a dance, returned to her house and set fire to her room. Another report in 1885 noted that a firesetter may actually remain at the scene of the fire, rather than running away.[13]

During the nineteenth century, "pyromania" became a very popular topic in the scientific literature. It was simply defined at that time as a chronic impulse to set fires. Anyone fitting that description was classified as "insane," which meant legally mad. This diagnosis apparently was frequently invoked for the simple symptom of a person's desiring to burn or set fires.

Not until a 1951 article did one psychologist draw attention to the many nuances of opinion over pyromania that had appeared in the early literature.[14] Terms such as *pyroptothymia*, introduced in 1863 and meaning the love of looking into a fire, were created by numerous authorities to categorize the incalculable number of symptoms attributed to this disorder, and a controversy over the psychodynamics of pyromania was born.[15] This early literature, replete with information on symptoms, categories, motives, types of fires set, and classification systems, began a trend in attempting to explain firesetting behavior. This trend continues to this day.

In the early half of this century, Freud and his psychoanalytical approach contributed to the literature on the subject. In a 1930 article entitled "The Acquisition of Power over Fire," Freud said that fire was symbolically expressive of libidinal and strong phallic-urethral drives. Freud felt that men, in attempting to extinguish fires with their own urine, symbolically engaged in a homosexually tinged pleasurable struggle with another phallus. He viewed the warmth radiated by the fire as evoking a similar state to that accompanying sexual excitement, and the form and motion of the flame suggested a phallus in motion.[16]

Claiming that sex was the underlying culprit in the preoccupation with fire, Freudians coined such terms as *urethral eroticism* (the centering of sexual feelings in the urethral zone) and *urolagnia* (the association of sexual excitement with urination or urine) as underlying motives associated with the thrill of igniting and then putting out fires. Connections were even made linking a sexual connotation with pyromania and the symbiotic relationship between the penis and urination and the fire fighter's powerful water hose.[17]

Although an emphasis on the sexual symbolism of fire continued into the 1950s, new perspectives began to question these urethral-erotic interpretations. Firesetting behavior came increasingly to be viewed as more complex in its root causes. As we document in our study, children who set fires exhibit a variety of behavioral problems. Feelings connected with sexual issues are just one of several explanations accounting for their incendiary acts.

Today, also, more comprehensive medical definitions of pyromania are being used to clarify this phenomenon. In fact, pyromania is the diagnosis *least* frequently used for firesetters, as they are more likely to be viewed by mental health practitioners as suffering from either a conduct disorder, an antisocial personality disorder, schizophrenia, or an organic mental disorder. According to medical criteria set forth in the *Diagnostic and Statistical Manual of Mental Disorders*, pyromania may be diagnosed only if the individual experiences "recurrent failure to resist impulses to set fires" and shows intense fascination with setting fires and watching them burn.[18]

The medical diagnostic manual lists several behavioral traits that characterize the pyromaniac, such as making elaborate preparations before starting a fire, being a regular observer at fires, setting off false alarms, and showing interest in fire-fighting paraphernalia. Case studies from our San Bernardino sample group, as well as our discussions with arson investigators, document these interesting patterns. Other symptoms listed in the manual include frequent alcohol intoxication, psychosexual dysfunctions, lower-than-average intelligence, chronic personal frustrations, and resentment of authority figures. Furthermore, according to the manual, the onset of firesetting behavior usually occurs in childhood.

The manual also stresses that young children's experimentation and fascination with matches, lighters, and fire may be a normal investigative part of their growing up, and not a prelude to firesetting behavior. The question arises as to how parents are to know when their youngster's fire behavior is merely curiosity and when it is indicative of deep-rooted problems. The categories set forth, as well as the behavioral characteristics that accompany each of the four levels of firesetting, should assist parents in making this important distinction.

Diagnosing the factors that lead to pyromania is pertinent to our book. Because the onset of pyromania usually occurs in childhood, and much childhood behavior can be modified, an assumption that is critical to our study can be made: If firesetting behavior is treated earlier in life, and if the treatment is effective, then the treated child can be prevented from continuing as a firesetter or a pyromaniac into adulthood.

Although the topic of pyromania is of interest to our study, it should be reemphasized that the vast majority of young firesetters are *not* diagnosed as pyromaniacs. In regard to terminology, *pyromaniac* is a term reserved for the most severely disturbed firesetters, who are the minority of firesetters. In our study, we focus primarily on those juvenile firesetters or arsonists whose behavior is categorized as either "playing with matches," "crying for help," or acting "delinquent." Only some of the "severely disturbed" firesetters are considered pyromaniacs.

Inevitably, the question arises: Why do they set fires? Why is our country experiencing such a wave of arson, and why is there an increase in the number of young arsonists? To ask why is to seek a cause and possibly to discover a cure.

As usual, there are broad assumptions to be made when studying irrational (or rational) human behavior. The etiology of the firesetting behavior of the young appears to be unique to each child or adolescent involved, although, as our research demonstrates, certain patterns appear to be prevalent.

The psychological development of a child does not occur in a vacuum. Therefore, let us consider two of the many changes that have taken place in our society that may have had an impact on the young. The use of fire, in its primitive form, has become more forbidden and regulated as our society has become more urbanized. Citizens are no longer permitted to burn garbage and leaves on their property. Opportunities to build recreational campfires are now often curtailed at most public parks and beaches, and even the areas designated for cooking are now restricted to a limited number of built-in barbecues. Public officials contend that the control of the use of fire has become a necessity for the protection of society in general.

The general lack of fireplaces in the modern home and the money needed to purchase wood to burn have made the use of primitive fire an upper-middle-class luxury item. Modern electric appliances long ago replaced the open hearth for purposes of everyday cooking, heating, or removal of unwanted waste matter. Now, fire in fireplaces has become a status symbol, an aesthetic delight used simply for mood or for visual and sensual enjoyment—particularly in those warmer parts of the country where fireplaces and fires are unnecessary for the purpose of heating, even during winter months. And in new home construction, fireplaces are included only in the costlier homes.

With the absence of fireplaces as an integral part of the family home, children are not as likely to be exposed to, or taught about, fire as a basic part of growing up. A child's curiosity about fire is not satisfied through the normal activities of her or his environment. The major exposure to fire for children is cigarette lighters and/or matches, which seem like adult toys for smoking, or occasionally for relighting a hot-water heater, an oven, or a stove. The diminished exposure to the primitive uses of fire may make it a more mystifying and therefore attractive element. Consequently, a youngster may become curious enough about fire to play with matches, although even with more exposure, the spark itself would elicit such a response in some children. Our first category of firesetters is this very group of young children whose parents never took the time to teach their youngsters about proper fire-safety measures.

Another factor that has been overlooked up to now is that the efficiency of modern fire fighting may actually work to promote fires. Perhaps society has become apathetic about the danger of fire because help when fires occur is often only a phone call away. Before the development of sophisticated fire-fighting personnel and equipment, the word *fire* struck fear into the hearts of rural and urban citizens alike. The great Chicago and San Francisco fires were lessons enough to make the nation conscious of fire safety. Proper fire use was taught at an early age, as it was crucial in protecting life and property. A means of suppressing fire efficiently and quickly did not exist in those days. Fire prevention and control, therefore, became paramount to human existence.

To the child of the past, who was taught to fear fire and was instructed in its proper use, we can compare the child of today, who may view a fire truck and sirens as fun and exciting. Or worse, he or she may view them as just another form of entertainment (like watching action programs on television), having little, if any, comprehension of fire's danger to life and society.

Since 1978, when the FBI reclassified arson from a Part II to a more serious Part I offense, law enforcement personnel have viewed arson as being on the same level of seriousness as murder and forcible rape. With this new classification, the *Uniform Crime Report* (UCR) policy on reporting arson has changed. Past policy had been to report only the most serious of offenses in multiple-offense situations, and often, arson was not even reported as a separate offense when, for instance, a homicide may also have taken place.

In the case of juvenile arson, there were many similar instances of underreporting, particularly in regard to the so-called burg-and-burn type of offense. This offense, a burglary followed by a burning to cover up the primary offense, would usually be reported only as a burglary. Now, in such multiple-offense instances, *all* occurrences of arson are duly recorded if they fit the criteria for arson (as we explain in Chapter 11). Because of this new pattern, the accuracy of the data collected by public officials on the number of arsons is of the highest level. Because of the practice of underreporting acts of arson in the past, however, it may mean that the increase in arson offenses is not quite as great as public officials claim.

The UCR bases its figures on those of participating law-enforcement agencies. According to these government figures, the most frequent targets of arson in 1981 were structures, which comprised 56 percent of the total of reported incidents. And residential property was the target in 59 percent of these structural arsons, with 42 percent of such offenses directed at single-occupancy residences. Abandoned or uninhabited structural property accounted for 17 percent of the structural arsons.[19]

Besides these structural fires, mobile property fires, such as fires in motor vehicles, trailers, airplanes, and boats, accounted for 23 percent of the arson, and the remainder of the fires were directed at other property, such as crops, timber, fences, and signs. Of all mobile property fires, motor vehicles comprised 91 percent.

The monetary value of the property damaged by reported arsons in 1981 was $914 million, and the average loss per incident was $9,399. Industrial and manufacturing structures registered the highest average loss: $59,358 per offense.

According to the *Uniform Crime Report*, all agencies reporting arson arrest and conviction data in 1981 showed only a very low 15 percent clearance-rate success nationally. This rate varied by city size, with rural counties having higher clearance ratios (21 percent) than either suburban counties (18 percent) or cities (14 percent). In terms of the type of property involved, the highest clearance rate recorded (34 percent) was for offenses against community or public structures, and the lowest (10 percent) was registered for motor vehicles. The UCR gives no explanation for these differences in apprehension rates by city size and type of property involved.

Arson figures for both the State of California and for the County of San Bernardino, our study population, followed national trends as reported in the UCR. Because of this similarity, our in-depth analysis of arson patterns in one county in the nation—as well as our profiles of those

juveniles who set the fires—can be viewed as representative of the larger national picture. By focusing on the
regional arson cases of one county in the nation, we hope
to shed some light on this shared, and frightening, societal
problem.

Chapter Three

BEHAVIORAL CHARACTERISTICS OF FIRESETTERS

Firesetting behavior in general has been scrutinized over a long period of time in the scientific literature. Over 130 articles on the topic had been published prior to 1890.[1] But in a 1980 appraisal of the research published in just the three preceding decades, it is lamented that comparatively little is known about the etiology or cause of firesetting, as so much of the accounts has been impressionistic and conjectural, based primarily on the authors' experiences with a limited number of firesetters and with limited statistical backing. Furthermore, much of this research has not been conducted in any systematic, and therefore reliable, fashion.[2]

Our study attempts to rectify some of these deficiencies of past research. Building on the broad scientific foundation that has developed on the study of firesetters over the past 150 years, we report in this and subsequent chapters some of the data collected on a group of young firesetters. In this chapter, the behavioral characteristics, as perceived by the parents of these young arsonists, are compared with the behavioral characteristics of nonfiresetters, again as perceived by their parents. This comparison will enable us to draw clear contrasts between the behaviors of these two matched groups of juveniles.

Furthermore, in this chapter, we examine three specific age groups of juvenile firesetters. Of interest to us are those behavioral characteristics that distinguish the younger children (four to eight years old) from the preteenagers (nine to twelve years old) and from the teenagers (thirteen to seventeen years old). By establishing a severity-level scale based on both the number and the frequency of problems, we shall be able to discern between the behavioral characteristics that distinguish the more serious and recidivist firesetting delinquents from the less serious and infrequent firesetters.

A checklist of eighty-four behavioral problem characteristics was one part of the diagnostic instrument developed by a team of six clinical psychologists and fire service personnel in the State of California.[3] Surveying the wide-ranging literature on the etiologies of arson behavior in young people, the team compiled a comprehensive list of every possible behavioral problem that had previously been linked to firesetting acts. With permission, we replicated portions of this test instrument in gathering data for our study. Copies of the questionnaires administered to both the parents of apprehended firesetters and the parents of a matched control group of nonfiresetters appear in Appendix A. A more comprehensive explanation of our sampling procedures for this portion of our study is also presented in the appendix. (Many of the statistical data and findings are to be found in this section of the book.)

For parents concerned about their own youngsters' becoming possible arsonists, this scale, and the behavioral problems checklist, should be helpful in pointing out critical trouble spots as well as patterns of delinquent behavior. By replicating these earlier findings, and by drawing a comparison between those behavioral problems that differentiate our two groups, we hope that our study will be able to assist parents in identifying important problem areas. And as we discuss in subsequent chapters, assistance and support are available to aid parents in working with their own troubled son or daughter who may appear to fit the pattern of either a potential or an actual arsonist.

The manual developed for the National Fire Commission, titled *Interviewing and Counseling Juvenile Firesetters*, provides fire service personnel with a means of recognizing problems in children that may lead to recurrent firesetting. The manual also illustrates how to interview firesetting children and their families; details methods and strategies for educating the curious firesetters and their families; explains in which ways to select children and families for professional mental-health assistance based on the severity of their problems; and notes ways to refer children and families for appropriate mental-health assistance.

One section of this comprehensive manual includes the portion we replicated for our study. This was the questionnaire designed to identify young children with potential problems and to classify them into three broad categories: the *curious* child, who may require nothing more than an educational program on fire dangers; the *troubled* child, who is reacting to stress in the family, and who requires counseling by fire officials and possibly by mental health professionals; and the *pathological* child, who is referred to a child psychologist or psychiatrist.

For the purposes of our study, we broadened the age range to include all juveniles under age eighteen. We expanded the identifying characteristics, reclassified the three categories, and added a fourth category. This added category was the *delinquent* child, who uses fire as a means of adolescent acting-out against authority, and who requires counseling, juvenile probation, and sometimes incarceration. Likewise, the severely disturbed or pathological older juvenile may be treated in an institution under the supervision of a regional training school.

Our four categories, therefore, were the following:

1. The curious or *playing-with-matches* firesetters
2. The troubled or *crying-for-help* firesetters
3. The *delinquent* firesetters
4. The pathological or *severely disturbed* firesetters

We should point out, however, that these four categories are loosely drawn and serve the purpose of allowing us to make some distinctions between both the age of the firesetters and the frequency and severity of their behavioral problems. Thus, for example, the younger firesetter is more likely to be categorized as either a "playing-with-matches" or "crying-for-help" firesetter, and the older juvenile is more likely to be categorized as either a "delinquent" or "severely disturbed" firesetter. But there are occasions where even the very young have engaged in firesetting behavior that is indicative of severely disturbed individuals. The parents of "severely disturbed" firesetters, moreover, view them as experiencing both a greater number of and greater frequency of behavioral problems than do the parents of members of the other three categories of juvenile firesetters.

Because many of the team psychologists who developed the classification manual were from Southern California, workshops were conducted for probation and fire departments in San Bernardino County on the manual's application as soon as it was published in 1979. By the end of that year, four county probation officers, under the supervision of Martha Lou Berkey, began to include components of the training manual in their case files and probation reports. In 1981, another local fire department with a new fire education and community outreach program was added to the list.

Four years later, by mid-1983, we had gathered the data for sixty-nine "complete" cases. A complete case included a detailed questionnaire on the background of the child filled out by the parents, as well as the eighty-four-item behavioral checklist, and, last, an interview with the juvenile arsonists themselves. These sixty-nine cases served as the data base for the firesetters' group to be discussed in this chapter.[4]

In 1972, psychologist William S. Folkman expressed a need to study firesetting behavior in normal children, or in the general population at large, so as to understand the behavior of young apprehended firesetters. Arguing that most fires are *not* the result of pathological behavior, Dr. Folkman claimed that studies of normal children would provide more comprehensive information for deriving an analytical theory of why children set fires.[5] In an early pilot study, Folkman and others found that of some forty-seven five- and six-year-old children in Berkeley, California, only two boys had been involved in agency-documented fires, although 60 percent of the boys and 33 percent of the girls had displayed a general interest in fire by requesting to light matches from time to time or had admitted to playing with fire materials without permission.[6]

As in that research, we also felt it important in our study to develop a comparison group. We specifically wanted to gather a matched group of juveniles who had *not* been apprehended by the authorities for starting fires so that we could compare the behavioral characteristics of the two groups. (The steps we took in collecting this comparative group are discussed in the methodological section in Appendix B.)

Because the fire administration manual was set up to administer the behavioral problems checklist to the parents rather than to the juvenile firesetters themselves, we also chose to administer the checklist to the parents of our nonfiresetters' control group so that comparisons could be drawn between the two groups. In accepting the parents' answers as pure fact, however, we recognize the fact that their responses may *not* be entirely indicative of their youngster's actual behavior.[7]

Even with this important limitation to the methodology of this portion of our study, we decided to proceed with an analysis and a comparison of the parents' perceptions of their children's behavior so that some distinctions might be drawn between the two groups. Hence, we compiled background information on the families of both firesetters and nonfiresetters. On the juveniles, we obtained information on such characteristics as age, sex, race, level of school, and sibling position or birth order; and regarding the parents, we learned about their current marital status, their ways of disciplining their child, and any recent changes and stresses that the juvenile might have encountered.

Our study shows that the juveniles in our two groups were closely matched. For instance, the median age for both samples of juveniles was eleven. Males accounted for over 80 percent of each group. Likewise, Caucasians were in a similar 80 percent majority in both groups. Further, the level of school and the order of birth were similar for both groups. In summary, our two groups of juveniles appeared to be nearly identical. A more detailed approach to their similarities, by percentage, may be found in Table B-1.*

However, we did note marked differences in the categories concerning parents and family. As becomes a common theme throughout this book, the families of juvenile firesetters are strikingly more disrupted and disturbed

---

* Tables numbered with the letter *B* are to be found in Appendix B.

than the families of nonfiresetters. The parents of fireset-ters reported over twice the number of recent disruptive changes in the family than did the parents of nonfiresetters (61 percent versus 28 percent). Changes reported by the parents of firesetters included, in descending order, a recent divorce and/or remarriage (20 percent), the death of a relative (13 percent), some other type of major change (13 percent), and the presence of a new baby (8 percent).

Linked to these disruptions was the fact that the parents of firesetters reported that their child had been under severe stress in the six months prior to the incendiary activity. In fact, over three-fifths (62 percent) of the fireset-ters' sample stated that the child *had* recently been under such stress, compared to only a few (10 percent) of the nonfiresetters' sample. Stress factors appear to play an important part in the etiology of arson.

Take, for instance, the case of "Jerry," an eight-year-old male Caucasian. Jerry had lost his mother one year before the fire incident. His father had been remarried for six months, and on the weekend before the fire, Jerry's grandfather had passed away. According to his father, Jerry had at one time been outgoing and verbal and had also had many friends. In recent months, the boy had become withdrawn and rarely played with his best friend. Further, Jerry had begun to fight with his one sister, disobeyed his stepmother, and had received low grades for the first time that year.

In our interview with him, Jerry stated that he day-dreamed about fire and dreamed about his deceased mother at night. The fire that Jerry set, in light of these disruptions, was highly symbolic. He ignited all the wedding pictures of his father's second marriage. Jerry, faced with these stresses, would obviously fit the criteria of our second category of firesetter, the "crying-for-help" arsonist. We thus recommended that Jerry see a mental health counselor.

Jerry's home situation, unfortunately, typified our San Bernardino firesetters' group. The death of a loved one or, more commonly, the separation or divorce of the parents, compounded these children's lives. For example, whereas 82 percent of the nonfiresetters' group lived with both natural parents, only 51 percent of the firesetters lived with both parents. Half of these troubled youngsters lived with one natural parent who was either divorced (20 percent), was widowed or separated (18 percent), had never married (6 percent), or had remarried (5 percent).

Earlier research has consistently noted significant family disturbances in the families of firesetters. One study, for example, reported a large number of deserting, alcoholic, abusing, and psychotic parents in the family history of firesetters.[8] In another study, 45 percent of the boys studied came from broken homes or were adopted or illegitimate.[9] Another study showed that firesetters were likely to come from families that were disorganized because of the absence of the father, the separation of the parents, or the severe psychopathology of the parents.[10] Further, in a comparative study of recidivist firesetters with nonrecidivist firesetters, the researcher found that the parents of recidivists reported lower levels of marital satisfaction.[11]

All of these earlier findings are supported by our study. And in subsequent chapters, when we discuss particular cases and categories of juvenile firesetters, we will discuss the pervasiveness of troubled family backgrounds among these young people. Family disruption, more than actual physical or even sexual child abuse, is *the* key factor in the background of these juvenile arsonists.

Our study confirmed the findings of some earlier studies, but it included more factors. According to the parents who completed the questionnaire, the firesetters came from families that had a parent missing, a marriage that was unhappy, and/or a setting in which one family member was currently in therapy. In addition, these parents indicated that neither the father's discipline nor the mother's discipline was effective with the troubled child. These parents also indicated that the child often ran away. Furthermore, a higher percentage of the firesetters had been adopted children than in our control group (13 percent versus 3 percent). We will have more to say about this pattern in Chapter 5.

In both of our study groups, the juvenile's mother (or stepmother) was the parent most likely to complete the behavioral checklist. In the case of the control group, although none had set fires that had got them into trouble with the authorities, some youngsters (17 percent) had been in trouble with teachers or police over other issues. And not all of the controls were fire-free. As in Dr. Folkman's study, mentioned before, some of the controls (18 percent), according to their parents, had *sometimes* played with fire against their parents' wishes, although none of these youngsters had frequently played with fire against their parents' wishes. By contrast, *all* of the firesetters' group had been in trouble with the authorities, if not for their firesetting, then for some other problem. Furthermore, the firesetters were viewed by their parents as both more *frequently* playing with fire (12 percent) and *sometimes* playing with fire (37 percent). Nonetheless, curiosity about fire was not confined to our firesetters who got into trouble with authorities. The frequency of playing with fire, however, did differentiate the two groups, as Table 1 demonstrates.

In terms of the discipline used, over half of both groups of parents indicated that they used two or more of the several forms of discipline listed, including spanking,

Table 1. Playing with Fire among Firesetters versus Nonfiresetters[a]

| | Plays with fire | | | Row total |
Group	Never	Sometimes	Frequently	
Nonfiresetters	63	14	0	77
	65%	36%	0%	53%
Firesetters	34	25	8	67
	35%	64%	100%	47%
Column total	97	39	8	144

[a] χ^2 (2) = 19.17067, $p \leq .0001$

yelling at, isolating, and withdrawing privileges from the child. One difference between the two groups, however, was that the parents of the nonfiresetters employed the withdrawing of privileges more frequently (36 percent versus 12 percent) than the other group. The parents of the firesetters, on the other hand, employed corporal punishment more frequently than those of the nonfiresetters (12 percent versus 4 percent).

These slight differences in punishment methods may be indicative of some socioeconomic differences between our two sample groups. As past research has shown, the parents of the lower socioeconomic strata more frequently use corporal punishment than parents from the middle socioeconomic strata.[12]

Of the eighty-four possible behavioral problems, thirty-three items statistically differentiated our two juvenile groups. That is, on close to 40 percent of the items listed, the parents of the firesetters indicated that their children exhibited problems that the parents of the nonfiresetters stated their children did not exhibit. (Several of the statistical findings presented here are shown in more detail in Appendix B.)

The two most distinguishing characteristics of the thirty-three problem areas were stealing and truancy. As Table B-2 indicates, six of the firesetters (9 percent), according to their parents, *frequently* engaged in stealing; twenty-six (38 percent) *sometimes* engaged in stealing; and the remainder (53 percent) were perceived as *never* having engaged in stealing. By contrast, no parents in the control group indicated that their offspring had *frequently* engaged in stealing. In fact, only ten (13 percent) mentioned that their child had *sometimes* stolen; the remainder (87 percent) indicated that their child had *never* stolen.

The patterns for school truancy were similar, as Table B-3 illustrates. For instance, twenty of the firesetters (30 percent) and five of the nonfiresetters (6 percent) were *sometimes* truant; five of the firesetters (7 percent) and none of the nonfiresetters were *frequently* truant.

Other school-related difficulties were also significant. As Table B-4 shows, the firesetters had significantly greater behavioral problems in school than did the controls. According to their parents' reports, 49 percent of the firesetters, compared to 39 percent of the nonfiresetters, *sometimes* had behavioral problems in school, and 21 percent of the firesetters, compared to 6 percent of the nonfiresetters, *frequently* had such school problems.

The patterns for learning problems in school were similar. As Table B-5 indicates, firesetters had significantly greater learning problems than nonfiresetters. Whereas 36 percent of the firesetters, compared to 40 percent of the nonfiresetters, *sometimes* had learning problems in school, nearly one-fourth (23 percent) of the firesetters, compared to only a few (5 percent) of the nonfiresetters, *frequently* had such difficulties.

In all three critical areas pertaining to school, firesetters exhibited more problems. They were more truant; they had a greater number of behavioral problems; and they had more frequent learning problems than nonfiresetters.

Other studies of firesetters have consistently found histories of poor academic performance, including severe scholastic retardation and significant grade failure. One psychologist, in an early 1940 study, found learning disabilities in almost half of her sample of young children.[13] In a later study, researchers found that most of the young firesetters (73 percent) had major school difficulties and that only 27 percent were able to study at their standard grade level.[14]

These difficulties with school, moreover, may be the culmination of a number of causes other than intellectual impairment. Environmental stress, anxiety, and lack of parental attention may result in learning difficulties. Whatever the reason, young firesetters tend to do poorly in school, tend to dislike the educational environment, and, as adolescent delinquents, tend to take out their frustrations on the school itself through their incendiary acts.

Another important characteristic that distinguished between our two sample groups was the parents' answers about whether their child was easily led by peers. As Table B-6 demonstrates, one-third (32 percent) of the parents of firesetters indicated that their children *frequently* were easily led by other children their own age, compared to only a few (7 percent) of the nonfiresetters. At the other end of the continuum, slightly more than one-fifth of the parents in both groups indicated that their children *never* were easily led by their peers; the remaining percentages said that their children were *sometimes* influenced by their own age mates.

A history of behavioral problems was another major distinction between our two juvenile groups. As Table B-7 shows, the parents of the firesetters indicated that their children had more *frequently* had long-term behavioral problems (15 percent) than did the parents of the non-firesetters (2 percent). The vast majority of nonfiresetters (88 percent), on the other hand, had *never* had a history of problems.

Other significant behavioral problems shared by the firesetters, and not by the nonfiresetters, included the following, listed by decreasing level of significance: lying, playing alone, impulsive, fighting with siblings or peers, impatient, out of touch with reality, jealousy, shyness, hyperactivity, stuttering, expressing anger, violent, and being a poor loser.

A youngster's playing alone may be indicative of the child's inability to cultivate positive peer-group relationships (although artistic children often play alone as well). As Table B-8 shows, firesetters were much more likely to be viewed by their parents as *frequently* playing alone (12 percent). By contrast, none of the parents of the non-firesetters observed that their child *frequently* played alone, although most of these parents (77 percent) did observe that their child *sometimes* played alone.

Hyperactivity also distinguished firesetters from non-firesetters. Fully one-fourth (25 percent) of the firesetters, compared to only one-tenth (10 percent) of the nonfiresetters, were viewed by their parents as being *frequently* hyperactive. These findings are given in Table B-9.

Many of these behavioral patterns, exemplified by our group of firesetters, have been documented in other studies as well. One psychologist explained the link between setting fires, hyperactivity, and aggression in the young. A child, unable to control impulses, may attempt to discharge tension through external means such as firesetting.[15] The researchers in another study of children found a direct correlation between firesetting, severe reactions of rage, and chronic hyperactivity.[16] Another researcher reported that firesetting coexists with a variety of antisocial

behavior, including stealing, sadistic behavior to young
siblings, and hyperactivity.[17]

Our study also confirms that firesetting in juveniles
is *not* a single, isolated behavior, but rather one accompanied by a range of behaviors that indicate psychological
and mental health problems. The cluster of thirty-three
problem areas linked with firesetting demonstrates the variety of problems of these juveniles.

Previous studies have also documented a cluster of
problems associated with firesetting, including running
away from home, truancy, stealing, destructiveness, and
aggression.[18] Furthermore, in a recent study, one psychologist noted that firesetting appears to be one of the
highest progressive stages of a career delinquent, and that
defiance, lying, wandering, and stealing are preconditions
for subsequent firesetting behavior.[19]

As we have seen, the firesetters had problems relating
to their peers. According to their parents, our young arsonists were more likely to fight with their peers, to be
easily led by them, to be poor losers, to experience jealousy, and to play alone. Moreover, they suffered from
being easy prey to negative influences from others, who
directly or indirectly influenced their delinquent behavior.

Previous research has also attributed both firesetting
and other delinquent behavior to problems in dealing with
social situations, as in relationships. In one study, the authors' analysis reconciled the contradictory behavior of the
two types of firesetters. They characterized one type of
firesetter as being restless, antisocial, and hostile toward
other children. The second type they perceived as being
anxious, withdrawn, and angry with themselves. Both
types showed hyperactivity and difficulty in peer relationships.[20]

From the previous research and ours, we would suggest that the firesetters differ from the nonfiresetters in

their need for "power enhancement." Feeling a lack of power or control in the home and the social environment, and with other people, these juveniles turn to setting fires as an expression of their great hostility and aggression, or as a response to parental abuse or neglect. As we will document in subsequent chapters, all three types of the more serious juvenile arsonists—the "crying-for-help," the "delinquent," and the "severely disturbed" firesetters—attempt to fulfill this need for power enhancement by setting fires.

It is also of interest to note that not all of the behaviors that we anticipated would differentiate our two study groups were found to be different. For example, early research had indicated that two of the major predictors of arsonist behavior were bedwetting and cruelty to animals.[21] Although we found that bedwetting differentiated the younger firesetters from the older ones, and that cruelty to animals differentiated those firesetters with a greater number of overall behavioral problems from those with fewer problems, neither bedwetting nor cruelty to animals clearly distinguished the firesetters from the nonfiresetters. In response to the question of whether the child wetted during the day, most of the parents of both the firesetters and the controls indicated that their child *never* wetted during the day (90 percent of firesetters and 95 percent of nonfiresetters), and the remaining percentages in both groups indicated that their child *sometimes* wetted during the day. No parent in either sample indicated that their child *frequently* wetted during the day.

In terms of cruelty to animals, although the firesetters expressed this behavioral trait more often than the nonfiresetters, this was not a statistically significant finding. For the firesetters, most of the parents responded that their child had *never* been cruel to animals (77 percent). Some children, however, had *sometimes* been cruel (16 percent) or had *frequently* been cruel (7 percent). By contrast, for the nonfiresetters, most parents indicated that their child had *never* been abusive (88 percent), with the others indicating their child had *sometimes* been cruel to animals.

Besides focusing on the behaviors of the two groups, we decided to further explore those behaviors that characterized the firesetters, themselves, by age group and by severity level. That is, we wanted to see which behaviors were more commonly shared by the young firesetters (ages four to eight), the preteenage firesetters (ages nine to twelve), and the teenage firesetters (ages thirteen to seventeen). Likewise, based on the actual number and frequency of behavioral problems, we wished to note which characteristics differentiated those youngsters with a greater number of problems from those with a fewer number of problems in each of the three age groups.

The *young firesetters* differed from the two older age groups on eight (11 percent) behavioral characteristics. In decreasing levels of significance, these traits were: destroys own toys, expresses anger by hurting self, is impatient, fights with siblings, stutters, is cruel to animals, bedwets, and thumbsucks.

Two of these patterns need further elaboration because the behaviors are commonly associated with firesetting.

As Table B-10 shows, the younger firesetters (ages four to eight) were more abusive to their pets than were the older children. Nearly 33 percent of these young children were *sometimes* cruel to animals, and 14 percent were *frequently* abusive. By contrast, cruelty to animals markedly decreased with age, as fully 90 percent of the youngsters in both of the two older groups were perceived by their parents as *never* being cruel to animals. But as we pointed out earlier, these findings must be viewed with some qualification because this behavior, when present in older children, is likely to occur away from the home environment and without the parents' knowledge.

A similar pattern held for bedwetting or enuresis. As Table B-11 demonstrates, the younger firesetters were more *frequent* bedwetters (18 percent), although some in the two older groups continued to be enuretic (9 percent of the preteenagers and 4 percent of the teenagers), a symptom that is more unusual in older children and indicative of stress and mental health concerns.

With the age group of four- to eight-year-olds, fifteen behaviors (17 percent) distinguished the more serious from the less serious arsonist in terms of both a greater number of and more frequent behavioral problems. A summary of all the behaviors shared by the more severe firesetters within each of the three age groups is presented in Table B-12.

Some of the behaviors exhibited by the more serious younger firesetters were, by decreasing level of significance: impatience, lying, hyperactivity, history of behavioral problems, disobeying, extreme mood swings, stealing, uncontrolled anger, destroying own toys, and expressing anger by hurting oneself.

The *preteenage firesetters* (ages nine to twelve) had eight behavioral characteristics that differentiated them from the younger and the older age groups. These children, for instance, were more likely to live in some type of family arrangement other than with both natural parents (34 percent versus 15 percent of the younger children and 9 percent of the older juveniles). Also, these preteenagers were more likely to fight with their peers, to be poor losers, to throw temper tantrums, not to play well with other children, to have nightmares, and to have poor or no eye contact.

Further, twenty-three behaviors (27 percent) were shared by the more serious preteenage firesetters. Some of these traits, by decreasing level of significance, were stealing, sleeping problems, bizarre speech patterns, cruelty to other children, out of touch with reality, being accident prone, and experiencing anxiety, depression, and stomachaches.

One important pattern that the preteenage firesetters shared was being easily led by their peers. As Table B-13 points out, the preteenage firesetters with a greater number of total behavioral problems were more frequently influenced by their peers than those preteenage firesetters with fewer total problems. This table typifies the percentages and patterns for the other characteristics shared by the serious preteenage firesetters as well.

The *teenage firesetters* (ages thirteen to seventeen), according to their parents, were differentiated from the two younger age groups in several ways, including health-related issues. These older juveniles, for instance, were more likely to experience vomiting, diarrhea, and constipation—all behaviors that are often caused by, and that are symptoms of, stress. Likewise, the older juveniles were more likely to be truant from school and in trouble with the police, as compared with the younger firesetters.

Furthermore, the more troubled older firesetters shared forty-four behaviors (52 percent) compared to the less troubled older juvenile arsonists. Thus, the *number* of behavioral problems shared by the more serious firesetters in each of the three age groups increased by age group (from fifteen shared behavioral traits for the four- to eight-year-olds, to twenty-three for the preteenagers, to forty-four for the teenage group). The older the juvenile, the greater the likelihood that the more serious firesetters would share a greater number of behavioral problems.

Rather than list all forty-four characteristics for the serious teenage firesetters, we will mention only the most prevalent ones. (For those readers who wish a more detailed analysis, we remind you that Table B-12 shows a summary of significant behaviors for each of the three age groups.) The more troubled older arsonists were likely to have a history of behavioral difficulties, to be out of touch with reality, to have strange thought patterns such as "hearing voices," to express jealousy, to suffer from severe depressions, and to have phobias.

Table B-14 shows the correlations for strange thought patterns for this group of severe teenage firesetters. *All* of the more serious teenage firesetters had a history of having such thought patterns, compared to none of the less serious teenage firesetters. Table B-15 shows a similar pattern for jealousy. Once again, the teenage firesetters with many behavioral problems were likely to have had frequent incidents of jealousy compared with those thirteen- to seventeen-year-old arsonists who had fewer overall problems. Similar patterns prevailed for the other forty-two behavioral problem areas that these more serious teenage firesetters shared.

In summary, as these patterns indicate, the older the juvenile firesetter, the more varied and complex the problem areas become. Further, in each of the three age groups of firesetters, there appeared to be subtle distinctions in terms of what behavioral problems they held in common.

Those young firesetters (ages four to eight) with numerous problems were more likely to express their anger and frustration by striking out at things close to them, such as the family pets, their own toys, and their siblings, as well as themselves. They also suffered from the physical symptoms of stuttering, bedwetting, and constant thumb-sucking.

The preteenage firesetters (ages nine to twelve) displaced this hostility onto others by fighting with their peers. They were poor losers and, paradoxically, were easily led by their peers. Among the physical symptoms in this age group were tics and twitches. They also had nightmares and poor eye contact.

In the teenage firesetters (ages thirteen to seventeen), who shared overall many more of the behavioral problems, frustration and aggression were expressed through such means as strange thought patterns, bizarre speech, and severe depressions. Further, these older juveniles experienced physical symptoms such as vomiting, diarrhea, and constipation.

Knowledge of these behavioral patterns for each of the three age groups of serious, and often recidivist, firesetters will assist us in our analysis of juveniles with conduct disorders who engage in consistent aggressive and antisocial behavior. As we explore the four types of juvenile arsonists in the following chapters, and as we analyze their case files and categorize their firesetting acts, we shall keep in mind these behavioral problems, which remain, for these youngsters, active, intact, and far-ranging. And though major family disturbances and stress may account for the often morbid and pathological reasons for their engaging in firesetting acts of violence, these behavioral symptoms, through proper mental-health intervention and counseling, can be addressed and, we hope, altered so that their danger to themselves and to society may be lessened.

As we have shown in this chapter, over one-third of some eighty-four behavioral characteristics differentiated our firesetting group from a closely matched group of non-firesetters. In the chapters to follow, we focus specifically on the firesetters themselves.

Chapter Four

"PLAYING-WITH-MATCHES" FIRESETTERS

Four young sisters in the Hollywood area were severely burned Friday when a parked car in which they apparently were playing with matches suddenly burst into flames, fire officials said. The father and grandfather of the girls suffered third-degree burns on their hands as they pulled the children from the blazing auto.

All four children—Venus, 5, Denise, 4, Jeanna, 3, and Judy, 2—suffered wide-spread burns on their hands, faces and arms, according to the Fire Department public information officer. The girls were taken to County Medical Center, where two were reported in critical condition and two were said to be in serious condition. The father, Jerry Ross, and grandfather, Al Ross, were treated and released.

Fire department officials said the girls apparently had been playing for some time in the car—which was parked with the windows rolled up in a driveway beside the home—when the father and grandfather heard a scream and saw that the vehicle was filled with smoke. When the men opened one of the car's doors, fresh air hit the smoldering upholstery and the vehicle exploded in flames, the officials said. During the few seconds that it took to pull the girls from the car, Wally Whet, a vehicle inspector for the California Highway Patrol, happened to drive by.

Mr. Whet said he grabbed a fire extinguisher from his car and rushed up to help, "but it was already too late . . ." "The car was burning so fiercely the extinguisher wouldn't do any good," he said. "The little girls were

41

stumbling around—burns on their faces, arms, legs and feet. They were in shock. They weren't even crying."[1]

Two small children were burned to death and their mother and brother injured in their home Easter Sunday morning in a blaze officials say apparently was caused by a child playing with matches.

According to county sheriff and fire authorities, fire fighters called to the two-bedroom house found the charred bodies of Cynthia Boren, 2½, and Randy, 11 months, in one of the bedrooms. Mrs. Deborah Boren, 25, and Robbie, 4, were rescued by neighbors before fire fighters arrived and were taken to the hospital. Mrs. Boren suffered first-degree burns on her left shoulder and back, smoke inhalation and multiple superficial cuts on her right leg and both feet. The cuts occurred when neighbors, who smashed a window to rescue her, pulled her through the broken window, according to a Los Angeles County sheriff's spokesman.

The spokesman said the mother was later transferred to another hospital where he said she was listed in guarded condition. Her son was treated there for smoke inhalation and released.[2]

The firesetters' group to be discussed in this and several of the following chapters was comprised of 104 juveniles who had been apprehended and processed by authorities for having set trouble fires in the four-year period beginning in mid-1979. Included in this group were the 69 juveniles discussed in the last chapter whose parents had completed the behavioral checklist.

In terms of age, these 104 juveniles were evenly divided among the three age groups. That is, one-third (35) were between the ages of four and eight, one-third (34) were between the ages of nine and twelve, and the remaining third (35) were between the ages of thirteen and seventeen. The median age for this group was ten, and their ages ranged from four to seventeen, with a fairly even dispersement among each of the ages. In terms of sex, males accounted for 91 of the 104 arsonists (88 percent). In terms of racial or ethnic background, Caucasians accounted for 94 of the firesetters (91 percent), followed by Mexican-Americans (6 percent) and blacks (3 percent). No Asian-Americans or other racial or ethnic groups were represented in this group of firesetters.

As to the actual number of fires set, these 104 juveniles ignited some 91 separate fires. Several of the fires had been set by groups of juveniles. Of these 91 documented fire incidents, 47 (52 percent) were set by white males who acted alone. The remaining incidents, however, reflected some distinctive patterns, which will be discussed in greater detail in subsequent chapters.

All 104 juveniles were apprehended in San Bernardino County, Southern California, and were processed through the fire-safety treatment program of the county's probation department or through the one fire department in the county that was staffed to work with juvenile firesetters.

San Bernardino County encompasses some 20,162 square miles and in 1980 had a population of 812,833 people. Within the confines of the county are vast deserts and mountainous areas. Along with these variances in geography and climate, there are both rural and large metropolitan communities served by fifty-three fire districts.

What made this county important to our study was the fact that it had the fastest growing rate of juvenile arson offenses in the state. Although representing only a small percentage of the state's overall population (3.4 percent), in 1979 the county reported 10 percent of all juvenile arsons, and these fires accounted for 43 percent of the property dollar losses for the entire state that year.

Further, these arson offenses in the county were increasing at an alarming rate. In 1977, the year in which reliable figures were first recorded, there were some 793 fires fitting the category of arson, resulting in property damage of $124,000. In 1978, the figures had risen to 977 suspicious or confirmed juvenile arsons and $171,000 in damage; in 1979, there were 1,044 youth arson incidents reported and a total damage of $2,700,000.[3] The average increase in arson by youth for the county during that three-year period was nearly 16 percent, compared to only 5 percent increase in crimes against persons and a 5 percent increase in crimes against property for the same time period.[4]

With these alarming figures for juvenile arson as background, we decided to focus on the arson problem in this county, where, because of the increased vulnerability to arson, public officials were receptive to the implementation of a program for interviewing and counseling juvenile firesetters. By focusing on the patterns of juvenile arson as they existed in this region where arsons were a growing problem, we expected that the results generated by our study could be applied to those other sections of the nation where juvenile firesetting was becoming a mounting public concern.

Each of the 104 juvenile firesetters (and their 91 fires) in our San Bernardino group was categorized as one of four types of arsonist: "playing with matches," "crying for help," "delinquent," or "severely disturbed." Placement in a category was based on a variety of criteria:

1. The composite score of behavioral characteristics for each juvenile firesetter as designated by the child's parent or adult guardian (as discussed in Chapter 3).

2. The type of fire set; the circumstances of the fire, including the written summaries of the arresting officers; and the case reports by the probation worker or fire safety personnel.
3. The age of the firesetter and a profile of any previous firesetting and delinquent behavior.

We should mention at the beginning that these four categories are somewhat artificial categories that were used for practical purposes to differentiate the young arsonists. Also, these categories are not cut and dried. The same subject might have elements of various categories, might overlap two or more categories, and might fit a different category, depending on the observer. But a practical method of differentiating these firesetters was necessary, if we were not going to throw up our hands in the air and say nothing could be done about them.

Accepting these reservations, we applied the above criteria to our 104 firesetters and found that 15 of them (15 percent) fit the category of "playing with matches," the focus of this chapter. The "crying-for-help" firesetters accounted for the largest group, with 41 arsonists (39 percent). The "delinquent" firesetters accounted for 36 (35 percent). And the "severely disturbed" firesetters numbered 12 (11 percent).

The two tragic fires reported at the beginning of this chapter represent the most common type of fires set by very young children, the "playing-with-matches" fires. Curious and fascinated by the spark and the igniting of a match, these children are not bent on destruction when they play with fire. Unlike the problem firesetter, these curious kids usually derive no satisfaction from the fires they ignite. Sadly, however, these young children may have only minimal parental supervision and little or no education about proper fire safety, so that the fires they accidentally set can be quite dangerous and damaging. Kids commonly have a natural curiosity about fire, but they need to be taught that fire is not a plaything or a toy.

In the very young child, curiosity regarding all objects and phenomena about the house is a very common and normal pattern. But according to several fire-safety professionals whom we interviewed, a surprising number of parents do not regard their child's playing with matches as a particular problem because these parents think that "all" kids play with matches, and that this is just a stage that youngsters go through.

To the contrary, we advise parents that it is never too early to begin to teach children about fire, and that a child's "innocent" playing with matches can lead to disastrous results—as the newspaper clippings show—or to a behavioral pattern that under no circumstances should be condoned by parents. Family members, instead, should intervene immediately when they discover a child playing with matches. All children require proper fire education from parents, from school, and from fire-safety personnel in matters pertaining to fire play and matches.

Research has indicated that children who *do* play with matches are more likely to come from divorced parents and disruptive family backgrounds. One study, for example, was conducted on 99 elementary-school children through the fourth grade. It distinguished between those boys who had deliberately set fires, those boys who had accidentally set fires while playing with matches, and those boys who had never engaged in any form of fire play.[5] The young boys who had engaged in fire play (either deliberate or accidental) were more often from broken homes than the boys who never played with matches. As we discussed in Chapter 3, the stress of a disruptive home life may make the child vulnerable to fire play. And this would be particularly true for those children who were neither educated in proper fire safety nor adequately supervised.

In this previous study, most of the fires that the young children set were in areas where they could not be easily detected by adults. Outside areas included the front or backyards or an open field adjoining the house. The more common inside areas included a closet, under a bed, the bathroom, the garage, a tool shed, and the basement.[6]

Other studies have been conducted on the location of the fires that these juveniles set. One study showed that younger children living in cities set fires in buildings, whereas children living in suburbs set fires mainly in fields.[7] Other researchers have reported that young children set fires mostly at home or nearby, but older children were more likely to be caught setting fires some distance from their homes.[8]

We observed similar patterns for our San Bernardino group of firesetters. The younger children (under age ten) generally set their fires in the morning close to and around home or on the way to school. The older juveniles set their fires some distance away from their homes, on or around their schools, and in the afternoon on the way home from school. These older teenagers were also more likely to ignite school property, open fields, cars, and abandoned buildings and shacks.

The fifteen firesetters in our San Bernardino group whom we categorized as "playing-with-matches" firesetters followed these general patterns of being younger, being curious about matches and fire, and setting an accidental fire.

One of our four youngest (all four-year-olds) firesetters was "Jay," a white male. Jay's parents were separated and his father's whereabouts were unknown. The initial complaint against Jay was filed by a neighbor whose palm tree, located between his own residence and the boy's home, had been accidentally set on fire by the boy's admitted playing with matches. According to this neighbor, the fire had been put out by the boy's mother shortly after it started. Though this neighbor did not wish to seek punitive damages, he called the police because he wanted a report made on the incident for insurance purposes. Damage to the tree was set at $700.

Another young firesetter was "Bruce," age six, who accidentally set his bed on fire while playing with a cigarette lighter he had got from his parents' room.

"Lucy," age seven, was another youngster who engaged in fire play. According to her mother, Lucy had been discovered striking matches in front of her two-year-old brother and letting him blow them out. A report was filed when the mother contacted the probation department about their fire-safety program. Part of the young girl's counseling required her completing a fire safety workbook and instructing her younger brother in proper fire-safety measures.

Another "playing-with-matches" firesetter from our San Bernardino group was "Nick," age eight. In the words of the boy,

> While I was walking home from school, I was met by a small boy who took us over to a small trailer, from which he took out some matches and gave them to me. I lit one to see if they were working. I then put it out and threw it down. I think it was out. The bush busted into flame and I ran away because I was scared.

Another example of a curious firesetter was "Bryan." This eight-year-old explained his reason for setting the fire:

> I was taking a walk with my friend and we stopped at an old joshua tree stump, and my friend started lighting matches and putting them into the stump. I wanted to do

it, too, so he gave me the matches and I did the same, just to have something to do.

One last example of a fire that appeared to be accidental in nature involved two boys who were unsupervised and should not have been playing with fire. According to the probation report, on the morning of the fire in question, "Fred," age eight, missed the school bus and walked to the home of his classmate, "Jim." Both boys watched cartoons on television for about half an hour and then decided to cook some popcorn. Obtaining a cooking pan, oil, and popcorn from the kitchen, the boys went outside to a campfire in a play fort they had dug out in a vacant field next to Jim's home. The started a fire with a cigarette lighter obtained from the house.

As the fire was burning, a wind blew sparks into the dry grass next to the fort and started a grass fire. Both boys tried to suppress the fire by throwing dirt and stomping on it, but the wind carried the fire away. Resolute to put out the fire, they went to the house and got the garden hose, but it would not reach the fire. The boys returned to the house with the pan, threw the popcorn out into the brush, took the pan into the kitchen, washed it, and returned it to the kitchen cabinet. The boys called the local fire department and then started walking to their elementary school.

Both boys entered the school without checking with the school office. When the school principal later questioned the boys about being tardy, he stated that he could smell brush smoke on the two boys. After some questioning, both boys admitted that they had started a fire. The principal notified the fire station, and the boys were eventually arrested for their fire. Fortunately, no structural damage occurred from this fire. The boys were assigned to a counselor.

In summary, we viewed these youngsters who constituted our "playing-with-matches" firesetters as being fairly normal kids. In many instances, they had been brought to the attention of the authorities when they had been referred to the probation department's counseling program, or because the parents had caught the youngsters playing with matches and wanted to provide them with proper fire-safety education. In other instances, the children had been recommended to the program because of parental neglect and lack of supervision at the home, and because school officials felt that the children needed some fire-safety instruction.

As we have seen, this type of firesetter is generally a younger child who is merely curious about fire or who has had an accident while playing with fire. The fires that these children set are usually close to home and are simplistic in that no solvents are deliberately used. In some instances, the children are merely mimicking their parents' behavior, such as striking matches to light cigarettes. The counseling strategy in working with these children and their families, as we will discuss in Chapter 12, is to assist the parents in teaching fire safety to their offspring.

The major safety concern for this "playing-with-matches" type of firesetter is that many young children in this group either are severely injured or die in the fires that they set, as the newspaper accounts will attest. In this regard, the young firesetters themselves are often the victims of their own fires. This is less often the case with the other three categories of firesetters, who take out their frustration on other people and on property.

Chapter Five

"CRYING-FOR-HELP"
FIRESETTERS

A 3-year-old boy whom his mother described as "kind of an ornery kid" set his younger two sisters on fire while she was next door, a San Joaquin County sheriff's officer said.

The boy was placed in Family Services Protection custody after the mother found the year-old twins by feeling her way through her smokey house. One baby was hospitalized in critical condition with burns on most of her body, and the other was in stable condition with leg burns. Mrs. Margaret Smith told investigators she had fed her son in the kitchen before going to visit a neighbor. She returned home fifteen minutes later to find the house filled with smoke. The boy apparently took a calendar off the wall, put it on the lighted gas stove and threw it into the babies' cribs.[1]

Not all juvenile fire play is a function of natural inquisitiveness, nor is it accidental. For many children, firesetting is viewed as a symptom of underlying emotional or physical stress. That is, there are some younger juveniles with emotional, psychological, and even physical problems that account for their firesetting behavior. These youngsters we refer to as our "crying-for-help" firesetters.

Psychologist Kenneth R. Fineman contends that three conditions have to be met before kids *deliberately* (as opposed to accidentally) set a fire.[2] First, as we have discussed, there appears to be a pattern of specific behavioral

51

characteristics that sets these youngsters at risk. Lacking friends their own age, stealing, truancy, and being hyperactive and moody are just some of their many behavioral indicators. Second, there needs to be a precipitating crisis that these juveniles are not able to handle adequately. Stressful situations include a disruptive home life, a recent divorce of their parents, an alcoholic and abusive father, the recent death of a relative or a pet, or a family that has moved numerous times.

These two factors alone, however, do not necessarily produce a destructive firesetter. On the other hand, a third condition, positive reinforcement for their incendiary activities, *is* likely to be the catalyst that produces a chronic firesetter. Once the juveniles gain some personal satisfaction and pleasure from their arsonist activities, there is a greater likelihood that they will become recidivists. Such satisfaction may be the parental attention that the youngsters receive for causing a fire incident; or the thrill of seeing the fire engines respond to their fires; or the approval of peers for being adventuresome and daring in igniting the torch.

The stress that these youngsters frequently experience falls primarily into two categories. The first is stress relative to a child's perspective of the world, which includes many events that would seem insignificant to adults. To a young child, such "earth-shattering" experiences as losing a pet, changing school or residence, not being permitted to attend a particular school function, or undergoing some other small, but very meaningful, event can be beyond the child's coping mechanisms. The concern is that the child will continue to deal with such frustrations and stress through repeated firesetting. In counseling, these youngsters are assisted with positive means of expressing their frustrations and anger, so that firesetting ceases to be an established and continued pattern.

The second category of stress common to these youngsters who deliberately set fires requires a more complex approach to treatment. As we will discuss in Chapter 8, stress resulting from physical, psychological, or sexual abuse, or incest or sexual exploitation, can often be treated only by removing or correcting the underlying cause of abuse. An abused or exploited child tends to feel angry and helpless, and the firesetting may be considered a distress signal—a call for some outside intervention to alleviate the situation. A failure to rectify this negative situation, coupled with the youngster's positive reinforcement from setting fires, will create a snowball effect for the youngster. As we have seen, the more serious and recidivist firesetters, as well as the older juveniles, begin to manifest a greater number of severe behavioral problems. When this happens, their firesetting behavior moves them out of the "crying-for-help" category into either the "delinquent" or the "severely disturbed" category.

With the younger "crying-for-help" firesetters, the firesetting patterns have not yet reached these critical stages, although, once again, the fires they set may have disastrous results. During the interviews with this younger age group of firesetters, the children often appeared to be angry and to feel helpless. Furthermore, they had set fires that had distinct patterns. For instance, the "crying-for-help" firesetters inevitably set their fires alone. Their fires were set fairly close to their homes. Quite often, they set fire to their own bed, their mother's clothes or bed, or their sister's hair or possessions. Thus, what is set on fire is often symbolic of their underlying anger. A youngster who deliberately sets his or her bed on fire, for example, is viewed as expressing an unhappiness with his or her current environment, as the bed usually represents security to a youngster. Further, the fires that these children set are usually small fires, and revengeful fires; moreover, the juveniles are often not even aware that their firesetting is a cry for help.

All 41 of the 104 juvenile firesetters in our San Bernardino sample whom we categorized as "crying-for-help" firesetters were under thirteen years of age. As it happened, the one-third (39 percent) of our sample that fit this category were fairly evenly divided between the young age group (four- to eight-year-olds; $N = 22$) and the preteenage age group (nine- to twelve-year-olds; $N = 19$). Once again, the vast majority of the firesetters in this group were male (36 boys and 5 girls) and Caucasian (37 whites, 4 blacks, and no Mexican-Americans).

Several case profiles of this category of firesetters should document the magnitude and range of these youngsters' stressful lives.

"Larry," a twelve-year-old white male, was apprehended for setting a vacant lot on fire by using kitchen matches that he had taken from his house. Recent changes in Larry's life included his family's moving to a new neighborhood, which necessitated a change in school for Larry. But more critically, one week before this fire, Larry had witnessed his father's running over and killing his younger sister. The father, angry with the boy, had shifted the land cruiser into reverse and had floored the accelerator, accidentally running over the sister, who was playing in the driveway. Needless to say, Larry felt an enormous sense of guilt for what had happened and was given psychological counseling.

A recent stressful death situation had occurred in the dynamics of "Aaron's" fire. This nine-year-old boy had experienced the death of his favorite, twenty-year-old sister two months before he lit his fire. At age five, Aaron had been an occasional "playing-with-matches" firesetter, but this time, he lit a rag and ignited branches on the ground on another person's property. Once the fire had started, Aaron ran home and attempted to call for help. Two weeks before the incident, according to the boy's mother, Aaron had told them he wanted to die so that he could see his deceased older sister.

In another case, a father's being recently sentenced to a five-year prison term for burglary helped to explain the firesetting behavior of a set of five-year-old twins. "Bob" and "Alan" and their mother had recently moved so that they could live closer to the prison where their father was being held. The boys' fire caused $15,000 worth of damage to a neighbor's home. Getting a pack of matches from a friend's car, the boys entered the house through the windows. They struck matches to a mattress and then tried to put the fire out. A passerby in a van rescued the kids from the house. The inside of the house was destroyed by the fire. According to the twins' mother, the boys' behavior had markedly deteriorated since her husband's imprisonment. This explanation could be considered a convenient excuse or a mother's rationalization. The boys, along with their mother, were recommended for family counseling.

Sometimes, the stressful situation is constant bickering and fighting between a child's parents. "Scott," a five-year-old only child, had a history of setting fires. According to his mother, the boy had set fifteen fires since the age of two. The mother disciplined Scott at least once a day. His most recent fire had been a blanket, which he lit while his parents were arguing on the phone. Currently separated, Scott's mother acknowledged that the boy's firesetting was a response to the parents' problems. It seemed clear to us, also, that Scott's fires were a combination of an attention-getting device and an angry response to his parents' marital difficulties. According to his mother, Scott wet his bed every night; had sleep problems, including nightmares and insomnia; and stared at fire for long periods of time. When questioned about his behavior, Scott responded that he "likes fire" and that he set his fires "in the morning, before Mom gets up."

"David," age five, set a fire because of anger and rage over his mother's constant discipline. According to newspaper accounts, David had a history of setting fire to his bed. This time he was successful, causing a fire that engulfed the apartment that he, his four-year-old brother, and his twenty-five-year-old divorced mother shared. At 2 A.M., David set his mattress on fire with a cigarette lighter that belonged to his mother, while the rest of the family and a visiting fourteen-year-old female friend were asleep. The mother and the boys escaped through the front door, but flames trapped the girl in the bedroom. As the room started burning, she broke the window and jumped about fifteen feet, breaking her ankle.

In a subsequent interview with the boy, David said that he had started the fire because he was mad at his mother for always yelling at him and spanking him. However, after the initial counseling with boy, and on subsequent visits to the probation officer, the mother stated that David continued to play with matches. Her response, which we considered completely inappropriate, was to take her cigarette lighter and, in her words, "burn the child's fingers." The boy and his mother were recommended for joint counseling, and the mother was advised in proper fire-safety and -prevention techniques (which we discuss in Chapter 12).

Another troubled boy who set a fire because of anger with his parents for constantly disciplining him was "Phil," age seven. This time, however, the parents appeared to us to have reason for concern. In the boy's own words, he had been "teasing and throwing rocks at the family dogs and picking up the cat by the neck and throwing him down." The boy felt, however, that his father often overreacted and was "quite mean to me and whips me." The boy, after one such beating, had set dry grass in a vacant field on fire. The fire had spread to the windbreak, where it fortunately stopped.

For "Pierre," age eight, the firesetting incident seemed tied to a feeling of being rejected by his father. Pierre is the third of three children and had recently had corrective surgery for a hearing problem. Since this surgery, according to his mother, Pierre had been less hyperactive, although he was still disciplined quite often. Pierre set ten fires, one of which was in his mother's bed. In each instance, the fires were deliberately set.

According to the mother, the boy got angry and frustrated when he felt rejected by his father, who showed an obvious preference for an older son. The father, a truck driver, even rebuffed his son when he offered to help work on the trucks. According to Pierre's mother, the boy's firesetting behavior always occurred when the father was on the road.

Another boy in our study set fires because of feelings of being abandoned. "Eric," age seven, was sent to live with his grandmother after the death of his mother and the hospitalization of his father following a motorcycle accident. Eric set a fire by igniting an old mattress in his grandmother's utility room. He felt that no one cared for him anymore.

"Kevin," age ten, was another example of a "crying-for-help" firesetter. Kevin, a black male, was the second of two children and was in the fourth grade. His father had died three years before the firesetting incident. Kevin is adopted. According to his mother, the boy had set ten previous fires to the garage, the side of the house, and his own personal items, as well as lighting matches in the fireplace against his mother's wishes. His most recent fire was setting a grass fire while playing with matches.

According to the probation report, Kevin had attempted to play the role of the hero by performing tasks to gain attention. At school, he was the class clown, and at home, he was the attention-getting problem child. According to his mother, the boy's firesetting had elements of "rescuing" the family. For instance, with a lighter found in his stepfather's desk drawer, Kevin once lit a fire under a second bed in his room, took his clothes off and got into his bed, and acted as if he had just awakened to inform his older brother of the fire.

The boy had severe behavioral problems, including frequent nightmares in which he was being chased by monsters. The boy had also run away from home two days before his most recent fire because of being disciplined for having stayed out past 9:30 P.M.

One of the most frequent causes of firesetting in young children is jealousy over a new baby. Four of our "crying-for-help" firesetters set this type of serious fire.

"Fred," age five, was in kindergarten and was the eldest of three children. He lived with his mother and stepfather. His parents had been divorced when Fred was one. Fred had set four fires. Most recently, he had set his middle sister's hair on fire. Although the mother felt that this incident had been an accident, the probation officer disagreed and categorized the fire as a "crying-for-help" incident. Fred's mother felt that the fire bolstered her son's feelings of power and self-confidence, as the boy was quite shy.

In an interview, Fred stated that the fires he had started "make him laugh"; that he dreamed about fires at night; and that there was a "fire on my back." As for his sisters, Fred gave the opinion: "Cheryl is three and she's mean, and Alice is a baby and she cries a lot." This five-

year-old ranked "The Incredible Hulk" as his favorite television character for being able to "turn green and throw
bad people."

With "Luke," also age five, jealousy of a new baby
and lack of parental supervision accounted for his firesetting. Recent stress included the return of his mother to
work after the baby's birth. In fact, the boy had set all four
of his previous fires while his mother was at work. His
most recent fire was on Christmas Day, when, according
to his mother, Luke felt that his baby sister was the "center
of attention."

With "Perry," age five, a second fire occurred the day
of his stepsister's christening. On this day, all the attention
was given to the new child, and Perry, who was visiting
his father and stepmother for the occasion, had been a
"total tyrant" all day. That day, he went into his bedroom
and ignited pine cones that he and his father had collected
together on a special excursion. At the time of the fire, as
the christening party was just breaking up, his stepmother
noticed him missing and found him in his room lighting
the pine cones.

Finally, "William," age four, the third child of four,
set a fire attributed to feelings of jealousy and sibling ri-
valry. This was at least his second fire. This time, he set
the baby's bed and bedspread on fire. His behavior so
alarmed his parents that they sent him to live with his
grandmother until they could figure out what to do with
him. In this fire, his two-year-old brother was badly
burned, and the family house was heavily damaged.

As we have just seen, these forty-one "crying-for-
help" firesetters share many common crisis and stress patterns. For one, the firesetting behavior occurred soon after
the divorce or separation of the parents. This happened
in 20 percent of the cases in this young age group and

category of firesetters. Second, the firesetting behavior occurred during a holiday or a family event when attention was focused on another child (in 20 percent of the cases). And third, the firesetting behavior often occurred after the recent death of a close relative (in 7 percent of these cases).

Two other intriguing patterns typified these youngsters. Several children in this "crying-for-help" group were adopted children (12 percent). According to one child psychologist we interviewed who specializes in treating young arsonists, adopted children start out with one strike against them. Even in more stable families, according to this specialist, it is difficult to know what deprivations the child might have experienced before adoption. Such deprivations set the (older) adopted child at risk. Feeling generally unhappy and not part of the family, these children, as they grow to maturity, often search for their natural parents. Without ways to express their feelings in positive ways when they are younger, moreover, they may resort to firesetting.

A last pattern is the unusually high number of bedwetters in this category and age group. As we observed earlier, enuresis was more common in our younger firesetters than in our older juveniles. Several researchers have delved further into the connections between firesetting and bedwetting. One study reports that 47 percent of thirty young boys who set fires were enuretic.[3] Another argued that bedwetting is merely the external expression of deep emotional conflicts, and that the child, in an act of "infantile regression," wets the bed as a means of drawing the mother's attention back to the child.[4] Another psychiatrist argued that enuresis is attributable to parental rejection, which causes the child to feel intense hostility toward the mother; by losing sphincter control, the child, in effect, is repudiating mother's toilet-training demands.[5]

A psychoanalytic bias is obvious in these interpretations. However, it is true that one-third of the boys in this "crying-for-help" category were frequent bedwetters. "Jim," age ten, was one of the older boys who continued to wet his bed at night. Jim was currently in the fourth grade but was doing poorly in school. He was the third of six children. He had been legally adopted at four months. His parents had had to discipline him daily, and his school nurse considered him hyperkinetic. Jim had set several fires, including the living-room couch, a grass field, and a recent trash fire. This fire he ignited with matches he had found on his way home from school, as his parents keep their matches locked up away from him. The reason the boy gave for setting the trash fire was "I wanted to see how it would go." He claimed that he dreamed about fire at night, and that in his dreams the whole family was in a house that burned. Jim was given psychological counseling.

It is quite obvious that "crying-for-help" firesetters are deeply troubled individuals and quite distinct from the "playing-with-matches" firesetters we discussed in the previous chapter. Whether their deliberate firesetting behavior is attributed to anger, jealousy, feelings of neglect and abandonment, the need to be a hero, or a need for power enhancement, these "crying-for-help" firesetters use fire as a means of resolving inner tensions and possibly as a (unconscious) strategy to bring about some desired change in the family environment. The fact that these children come disproportionately from troubled families, where separation and divorce are commonplace, or that several of these youngsters, in being adopted, had been "given up" by natural parents, leads us again to emphasize the significance of broken families in these young children's lives.

Chapter Six

"DELINQUENT" FIRESETTERS

Two 13-year-old boys have been arrested for investigation of malicious arson in connection with setting 67 fires in the San Fernando Valley over the last six months. Los Angeles County Fire Department investigators say one youth confessed to touching off 38 blazes and the other to 29. The boys, who were not identified because of their age, are being held in juvenile placement homes while awaiting trial. According to authorities, they belonged to a "Pyro Club" which operated out of their junior high school.[1]

The burning of a storage bungalow at Roosevelt High School was blamed on arsonists Friday by Principal John Rogers, but he said he was positive that the incident had nothing to do with Friday night's football game with arch-rival Garfield High. Mr. Rogers said he feels, rather, that the blaze that caused more than $100,000 damage late Thursday was probably set by the same non-students he suspected of painting graffiti on an adjoining bungalow last weekend. Athletic equipment, ROTC uniforms and booster club material were reported lost in the fire.[2]

A 17-year-old Mexican national was booked for investigation of murder and arson in a fire that killed 24 people, including several of his relatives, authorities said. Edwardo Enriquez is suspected of setting fire to a 55-year-old apartment building because of an argument with his uncle, the police chief said.

"He indicated he had a fight with his uncle who was unhappy about his being a gang member, smoking pot and hanging around with gang members," Chief James Woods said. "He was spray painting graffiti on walls and those

63

kinds of things, and his uncle apparently embarrassed him among other gang members."

Twelve children were among the victims of the weekend fire that raced through the building. Eighteen of the victims died at the scene, the others died later. Charred bodies were found crammed in third-floor hallways and in the rear stairwell near exit doors, evidence of the panic that swept the building. The suspect allegedly used a petroleum product, which officials would not identify, to ignite and feed the flames, police said.[3]

According to fire-safety personnel, this category of "delinquent" firesetters is often the most troublesome. Not only do these youngsters share the emotional disturbances of the younger troubled firesetters, but now, as older children, they are granted greater freedom and independence, and they experience heightened peer pressure—all of which contribute to their arsonist activities.

Part of the problem in curtailing this type of juvenile arson—or *malicious mischief*, as it is officially termed—is the difficulty that arson investigators have in proving there was "probable cause," meaning that a particular juvenile *deliberately* set the fire. One fire investigator informed us that he knew of incidents where kids had been "terrorizing the neighborhood" for years by setting cars on fire, slashing tires, and breaking windows. But no arrests could be made because the neighbors, who suspected who the culprits were, either were too afraid to press charges for fear of reprisal or had not actually seen the juveniles "in the act" of committing the offenses.

According to another arson investigator of one Los Angeles County fire department, many of the juveniles who set these delinquent-type fires are from "perfectly good white middle-class homes." Although in their early teens at the time of their arrest, these kids have often had a history of setting suspicious fires since they were six or seven. In the words of this spokesman, "If you can stop them when they're young enough, then you can prevent them later on down the road. Most of these kids are 'ring' wise. They know if they keep their mouths shut, there's no way we can prove anything [unless they are caught "in the act"]. They're just 'little bad asses' is what they are."

The firesetting behavior of these "little bad asses"— or "Juvenile Vandalism—Type II," their official law-enforcement classification—can be differentiated from the other three types of juvenile arsonists. These youngsters set fires as acts of vandalism, as a cover for other crimes, as a way of creating excitement, or for the pure enjoyment of destroying property or objects. As our San Bernardino case profiles show, the "delinquent" firesetters are typically influenced by their peer group or gang. They set fires to gain group acceptance or approval, and they are likely to torch objects and structures that appear safe to burn without their being caught or without anyone's being hurt.

One arson investigator whom we interviewed noted that distinctions could be drawn between the preteenage (ages nine to twelve) and the teenage (ages thirteen to seventeen) delinquent firesetters. In his opinion, the preteenager generally sets smaller fires and sets these fires for fun and amusement, whereas the older teenager sets larger fires and sets these fires because of peer influence.

Arson investigators for the forestry service in San Bernardino County concur that a large number of wildland brushfires are set by preteenagers who want the thrill of seeing all the fire-fighting equipment and the smoke and flames, as well as having the power to bring the paraphernalia onto the scene. The youngsters do not think about or foresee the potential damage that such fires cause.

A case in point: A twelve-year-old boy was convicted of causing a 1,600-acre fire that burned seventeen homes and caused $1.2 million in damage. The fire investigators felt that the youth had been more negligent than malicious in intent. In the words of the battalion chief who apprehended the boy:

> They want to see the circus come to town. All the activity—the trucks, the aircraft—appears glamorous. There is lots of smoke and action. The fires are very spectacular. People want the excitement. They actually don't think they're going to hurt anybody.[4]

The following newspaper account further illustrates the adventurous aspect of these preteenage delinquents' firesetting behavior.

> Sam, age 11, and a friend were walking home one spring day when "both of us got the idea to see what the truck would do if it burned. We planned for about a week, and then we finally did it."
> They set fire to a tank truck that appeared to have been abandoned in an orange grove near their home. They knew it was wrong, but they put that out of their minds. The boys sneaked some matches out of their friend's house, walked to the grove and lit a fire under the truck. When the flames got out of hand, "I felt kinda sick," Sam said.
> The two ran back to the friend's house and told an older brother, who called the fire department. The boys returned to the grove to watch fire fighters put out the blaze, which had spread and damaged four citrus trees. While there, they were questioned by a fire fighter. "We told a fib about two boys," Sam said, his eyes downcast. But the fireman saw through the story, and the boys ended up at the police station.[5]

One San Bernardino probation officer had a novel way of working with these preteenagers. Part of the boys' counseling program consisted of writing a detailed account of the events leading up to the fire, as well as an explanation of how the fire was set. The purpose of this assignment was to enable the firesetters to take personal responsibility for their actions and, furthermore, to realize the forces that had influenced their behavior.

One such account, written by a twelve-year-old boy, was as follows:

> Me, Tom, Bob and Jim were in Tom's home. Jim and me went to the "Country Store" to buy us some candy and gum. On the way back we found a tennis ball, so me and Jim took it to Tom's house.
>
> When we got there we put it on the porch and went into the house. We all were trying to think of something to do, so we got the idea to get the tennis ball and light it on fire. Bob had some airplane fuel, and Jim had a lighter. Bob put some fuel on the ball and he lit it on fire. Then all of us started kicking it around on the porch.
>
> Someone kicked it out and I went after it and put it out. Then I brought it back and we lit it on fire again. Then someone kicked it out again and lit a tree on fire across the street. Me, Bob, and Jim tried to put it out. Tom was gone when we lit it the second time.
>
> Anyway, we got pots, bowls, and pans and put it out before it spread. Then Bob and Jim left. Then the fire marshal came and asked me a lot of questions. The reason we did it is because we didn't think it would catch anything on fire. It was sort of a challenge.

As these examples demonstrate, the primary motivation for such fires may stem from a simple need for excitement and adventure. With the older teenagers, however, the motives become more complex, and the fire incidents take on a decidedly more "delinquent" character.

According to the arson investigators whom we interviewed, the older teenage firesetters generally have had a history of antisocial behavior. The fires they set are usually larger, premeditated, and, depending on the juvenile's level of sophistication, more "professional" in terms of the type of incendiary device used. Sometimes these teenagers set fires to cover up other crimes, such as vandalism or burglary. Or their fires become a game of attempting to outwit the authorities for the purposes of fun or excitement.

As we have stated, one-third of the juveniles in our San Bernardino group were categorized as "delinquent" firesetters. Most of these youngsters were males (83 percent), although the delinquent females shared special characteristics (a point we develop in Chapter 8). A majority of the delinquents were Caucasian (83 percent), and the remainder were Mexican-American. There were no blacks classified as "delinquent" firesetters in this particular group. Further, all of the juveniles in this category were over the age of nine with most ranging between the ages of thirteen and seventeen (75 percent).

Fires set by delinquents are usually set in groups, as the actions of "Paul," age thirteen, suggest. According to his probation officer's report, on a Sunday afternoon just after the start of school, Paul and a friend, "Frank," took a city bus to a shopping mall to see a movie. They met two girlfriends, "Rebecca" and "Sandra," and instead of going to the movie, they stayed around the mall for several hours, only to leave when one of Sandra's friends got into trouble for shoplifting.

Paul and Frank and the two girls took a bus home. Between the bus stop and their homes, they passed an abandoned car. Paul suggested that they set the car on fire, whereas Frank said that it was a "dumb" thing to do. Paul dropped a lit match through an old burn hole in the front seat. The match went out. He then had Frank hold a piece of paper, which he lit. He threw the paper into the driver's seat and the seat caught fire. The four juveniles then ran down the street and into a vacant lot. Paul set a bush on fire. A car was coming down the street, so the four ran to Frank's house. They later went to Rebecca's house, where Paul's father, having been informed by a neighbor of his son's actions, picked them up and transported them back to the scene of the auto arson, where they confessed to police. Paul could think of no other motive than that he wanted a "little excitement."

According to his probation report, Paul had had a history of truancy. His parents stated that the boy got into trouble when he was in the company of Frank. The youth had had a history of bedwetting until he reached puberty. There was also frequent family discord in the home. The probation officer recommended that Paul receive counseling as well as work to pay restitution to the owner of the burned car.

Another case involving two delinquent boys and a serious fire was that of "Donnie," age fourteen, and "Walter," age fifteen. These teenagers were nearly overcome by smoke in a fire that they set in an abandoned grocery store. According to the probation report, on the day of the fire Donnie went to school, attended his homeroom class (for roll call), and then "ditched." He drank a half pint of rum and went to the park and sat around. Donnie had been drinking heavily for the past year before the fire. In the early afternoon, he met Walter, who was also ditching school.

About 2:30 P.M., they went to "Sam's Market," a building which had been vacant for seven months. On this day, the door, which was usually open, was nailed shut, so Donnie kicked it open and the two entered the building. Once inside, Donnie made a torch so they could see. According to Walter, Donnie saw that there were cans of gasoline inside, poured the gasoline on three small boxes, and lit the boxes with matches that he had shoplifted from a "Stop-and-Go" market a week before. At this point, the boys' recollection became hazy in describing the events.

Apparently, the fire quickly got out of control, and both boys were barely able to escape the burning structure.

According to their probation report, both boys had a history of behavioral problems and family disruption. Donnie's mother, who had been recently divorced, claimed to have difficulty in handling her son. Since this fire incident, however, the teenager had become a "Christian" and was no longer "running with a bad crowd." Walter's parents observed that their son was more delinquent during periods of their marital discord. Walter's father worked the late-afternoon shift as a janitor, and the mother worked the same swing shift on alternate days as a nurse's aide. An older sister was usually at home. Three months before this fire incident, Walter had run away from home following a parental disagreement. He had come back a week later on his own. According to his mother, the boy had never got along with his dad, and his dad had often hit him when he was small. The probation worker suspected that the child had been abused as a youngster.

Both boys were recommended to seek counseling. Walter was placed on informal probation, and Donnie, who had lit the fire, was sentenced to formal probation, as well as "civil restitution"—work service in the community.

Another teenager with a history of parental physical abuse was "Harry," age sixteen. Harry was diagnosed as a chronic firesetter with a history of psychiatric treatment. Part of his difficulties stemmed from a physical deformity. Harry was born with severe curvature of the spine, which limited his functioning and caused a noticeable deformity. Very shy and withdrawn, he seldom communicated with others. For the past year, he had been receiving weekly psychiatric help, but this had stopped several months before the fire incident because the boy, in the words of his father, had made "substantial progress."

Harry was viewed as being very immature for his age. Like several other teenage firesetters in our group, Harry's closest friends were all three or more years his junior. He had repeatedly stolen money from his parents and had taken candy and other inexpensive items from stores. In the company of two other thirteen-year-old boys, Harry lit a pile of leaves in a vacant field. The fire got out of control and did considerable damage. The boys were caught fleeing the scene.

When contacted by the probation officer, Harry's parents stated that, when other children picked on the boy at school, he got nervous and upset, which culminated in his setting fires. In other words, he used fire as a means of displacing his aggression and frustration. The probation officer also felt that the son had experienced some physical abuse from his father. The boy stated that his father often hit him on the head. When confronted with his son's statement, the father responded, "I sometimes do things to make Harry angry so I can see my son's physical strength." The probation officer recommended continued therapy for the boy.

Several juveniles in our San Bernardino group were labeled as incorrigible by their probation officer and clinical psychologist. One such pair of delinquents were brothers: "Alfredo," age thirteen, and "Ricardo," age fourteen, two of eight natural children and one stepsibling. These two Mexican-American boys lived with their mother and her boyfriend of three years. The boys had not seen their natural father in four years, and according to police reports, all of their older siblings had been in some sort of trouble with the law. One twenty-two-year-old brother had recently been released from jail and had moved to Mexico.

The brothers were diagnosed as having an "oppositional disorder" because of incorrigible attitudes and belligerent behavior toward authority figures. In a series of psychological tests administered to the two boys, Alfredo wrote, in an Incomplete Sentences Test, that his nerves "sometimes twitch when I'm scared," and that what annoyed him most about his friends was "that they are all thieves." Ricardo wrote that he sometimes wished he "were dead," and that his father "should have stayed with us."

Both boys were suspected of being affiliated with a gang, a fact that their mother disputed. They set fire to a shed housing recreational equipment in a park frequented by a rival gang. The boys were observed by residents near the park and later questioned by police.

One interesting note to this case was that Alfredo expressed to his counselor a vocational interest in becoming a fire fighter. As his clinical psychologist recorded, "The link between the present charge of arson and a desire to become a fire fighter are explained in the similar dynamics often seen in juvenile firesetters, which suggest that Alfredo is seeking a father image or relationship and a male model that he can emulate." (We will have more to say about this connection in Chapter 10. At that time, we will present data from our study of one fire department, which showed that over half of the fire fighters had themselves, as youngsters, set trouble fires. Alfredo's situation, it appears, was not unique.)

The greatest number of fires (37 percent) set by the "delinquent" firesetters in our San Bernardino group were school-related. Further, school-related fires accounted for 14 percent of the fire incidents in our study group.

School-related fires are by no means limited to this region of the country. Arson strikes in all school districts, from the inner city to rural areas. According to government figures, arson is the most expensive of crimes inflicted on our school systems. A recent Senate report estimated that public schools in the United States lose close to $600 million a year to vandalism, 40 percent of it by arson.[6]

According to Los Angeles city fire departments, every year arson fires in the city school system cost taxpayers $1.5 million in damages. And according to the state fire marshal, virtually every junior high school in California has an arson fire once a year. One recent survey by the National Fire Protection Association found that 76 percent of school fires are caused by arson. The most popular place for starting a fire is the unoccupied classroom, followed by storage rooms and offices. The prime time for starting these school-related fires is between 10 P.M. and 6 A.M.[7]

Some recent success in combating school arson has occurred in the Los Angeles Unified School District. Working full time as a district arson investigator, one officer has developed a number of techniques that have worked to solve half of the school arsons committed. Among the techniques are extensive use of stakeouts, peer pressure on those who commit the majority of arsons, pattern recognition of the arson offenses, and the questioning of everyone who may know something about the case.

According to this investigator, most of the fires are set either by students who attend that particular school or by youngsters in the immediate neighborhood who have a grudge against someone at the school. Most fires are set on the weekends, when kids, with nothing better to do, break into school and then set a fire to cover up their break-in.

False alarm offenses have also been found to be committed largely on school grounds. In a 1972 study of false alarm offenses in San Diego, it was found that the vast majority of the offenses were committed by white, male youngsters from various socioeconomic backgrounds. Most of these offenses occur during the school day or at times such as lunch break, when the youngsters have minimal supervision. A large percentage of these false alarms were turned in expressly to disrupt classroom activities.[8]

One school district in San Bernardino County compiled records of all school-related fire incidents for a six-year period in the mid-1970s. The "Liverpool" Unified School District reported a total of 536 school-related fire incidents in the years 1973–1979. The median number of offenses for this period was 89, with a high of 107 fire incidents recorded in 1979, the last year in which figures were compiled.

In analyzing these data, we noted that the median age of the juveniles apprehended for these fire incidents was fourteen. Nearly all (91 percent) of the episodes involved males. Five types of fire incidents were distinguished. The most frequent offense (nearly half, or 46 percent) was possession of, or igniting, firecrackers or explosives on school grounds. Off-campus fires, including grass fires and brushfires near school grounds, accounted for the second highest incidence (23 percent). The three remaining offenses included, in descending order, "playing with matches" on school grounds (14 percent), setting fire to school property (9 percent), and fire incidents that were unclassified (8 percent).

The State of California has laws that make it illegal to possess any of the following fireworks: firecrackers, M-80s, cherry bombs, bottle rockets, aerial rockets of any kind, Roman candles, and any fireworks that explode or are shot into the air. Even with these restrictions, however, children do gain possession of fireworks. According to fire authorities, the youngsters often purchase them with (or without) their parents' approval during their vacation travels to other parts of the country or to Mexico, where the sale of fireworks is legal.

According to one authority in the San Bernardino area, brushfires are commonly started by youngsters who have moved away from an urban area. In their former surroundings, they played with matches and fireworks, and nothing happened. But now, in new tract homes, surrounded by grassy hills and dry vegetation, their mischief can lead to disaster. Brushfires are often set by youths launching small rockets from soda bottles.

Such fire-related problems are not unique to California. According to government figures, during a recent three-year period there were over 2,494 structure fires caused by fireworks, resulting in losses exceeding $10 million. Three-quarters of the structure fires were due to bottle rockets that caused roof fires.

In addition to the monetary losses caused by fireworks, during 1979 there was a total of 958 firework-caused injuries. Nearly half of these injuries were caused by firecrackers and involved lacerations to hands, feet, head, and eyes; burns about the face; and acute hearing losses and external ear inflammation. Injuries by age groups for juveniles in 1979, according to government figures, were as follows: age five and under (47 injuries), ages six to thirteen (133), and ages thirteen to eighteen (109).[9]

In analyzing the data on these 536 fire incidents of the Liverpool Unified School District, several distinctive patterns emerged. For one, males and females were involved in different *types* of fire incidents. As Table B-16 shows, nearly half the fires ignited by boys were caused by fireworks (49 percent), followed by off-campus fires (29 percent), and "playing-with-matches" fires (22 percent). By contrast, nearly half the fire incidents involving girls were off-campus fires (46 percent), followed by "playing-with-matches" fires (35 percent), and fireworks (19 percent). Further, the girls were generally older than the boys when they were involved in fire incidents.

Differences in *age* were also found with respect to the types of fires set. As we would expect, the younger school-aged children apprehended in the Liverpool schools had been caught for "playing with matches"; the preteenagers had more varied fire play; and the older teenage delinquents were more often involved in possessing or lighting fireworks. These patterns are presented in Table B-17.

With respect to our own San Bernardino sample group, the median age for the juveniles who set school-related fires was fourteen, although playing games that deal with the topic of fire occurs in much younger children, as this school jump-rope rhyme indicates:

> Had a little clothing store
> Couldn't make it pay
> Asked my wife what to do—
> She told me right away:
> "Take a can of kerosene
> Put it on the floor
> Take a match, give a scratch
> No more clothing store."
> How much money did we collect?
> $1,000, $2,000, $3,000 . . .[10]

One typical school-related fire incident was the case of three fourteen-year-old males who cut a math class to smoke cigarettes and, out of boredom, set a eucalyptus tree on fire on the school grounds. All three teenagers were poor students. "Kurt," the ringleader of the trio, had been kept back in kindergarten and third grade and was now repeating seventh grade. A second boy, "Randy," had been in trouble with the authorities for possession of marijuana, and his mother, when summoned by school authorities, arrived drunk and crying, saying that she did not know what to do with her son. The probation officer recommended that Randy be placed in juvenile hall because he was "incorrigible" and because his mother was unable to care for him properly. The other two boys were placed on probation and suspended from school for one week.

Another case typifying the delinquent school-firesetter was "Sean," age fifteen. Sean was in the tenth grade and had a history of lying, stealing, temper outbursts, truancy, and marijuana use. His parents had placed him in a military school in Missouri for purposes of control, but the boy was expelled after two years because he was caught with marijuana. His parents had adopted him when he was seven months old. He had had a history of firesetting. When he was three years old, he had set the house on fire, and his two sisters had been badly burned. He had also set backyard leaves on fire. Before his arrest for setting an off-campus fire, the boy and a friend had been suspected by school officials of setting four fires, and local police suspected that they had been involved with three non-school-related fires as well. According to his probation officer, Sean's parents were unable to properly restrain the teenager, and in his present home environment, the juvenile was able to do as he pleased. Both parents worked, and there was no one to supervise Sean most of the time.

In general, the motivation for most on-campus school fires is revenge, spite, or disruption of classroom activities. The fires are set most often in closets, in classrooms, and in wastebaskets under the teachers' desks. The boys responsible for these fires are generally known troublemakers, and most often, their fires are set following a punishment by a teacher or other school authority.

According to Aetna insurance fire investigators, school fires set by girls are less aggressive than those set by boys and are generally set to gain attention or to prevent a test from being administered. The girls are often observed to be the first to offer to clean up the mess from the fire and to give sympathy to the teacher.[11]

Our San Bernardino group exhibited some of these patterns as well. Two teenage boys, for example, set their fire out of spite. According to "Frank," age sixteen, he and a friend, "Carlos," also sixteen, set the cheerleader's banner on fire "to make it more exciting for everyone," and because "those kids are always popular and get to do things." Carlos acted as the "lookout" while Frank set fire to the senior plaza at their high school on the day of a rally and football game. The fire was set early in the morning, and the banner, as well as one school wall, was badly burned.

Both boys followed the pattern of "delinquent" firesetters. Frank, for example, had a history of firesetting. In his sophomore year, he had set a trash can on fire at school after, according to the boy, his father had been drinking. Frank had learning difficulties; he had been in special classes and had been truant much of the time. He also suffered from stuttering. Carlos also had school problems and a history of health difficulties, including a recent hospital stay to repair his rectum. Both boys were suspended from school for their fire.

"Keith," age sixteen, set off a smoke bomb at his school "for excitement and so they would have to dismiss school." Like the others, Keith came from a disturbed family and had been truant from school. In the interview, Keith admitted to a history of playing with firecrackers, which began when he was eight years old, when he would, in his own words, "blow-up ant hills with firecrackers for the hell of it." Keith, like the other juveniles, was suspended from school for his prank.

"Rosa," age ten, was another example of a firesetter who had learning problems. Rosa was in the fourth grade and had lived with her aunt and uncle because her natural father was in jail and her mother was dead. Rosa had been in trouble for the past school year, during which she had begun special-education classes. In her interview, Rosa, a Mexican-American, stated that she did not like school "because the kids tease me for being stupid." She set toilet paper on fire in the school bathroom and was suspended from school. She had previously set her uncle's backyard on fire.

By far the most serious school-related fire offense occurs when the juvenile actively plans to set a destructive fire or enters the school grounds at night or on weekends, when no one is around to assist in putting out, or reporting, the fire. Four of the firesetters in our San Bernardino group deliberately set their schools on fire.

"Raul," age fifteen, a Mexican-American, along with a girlfriend, broke into his high school late one school night and set the school on fire. Raul was the youngest of six children, and his parents had separated soon after the boy was born. Raul had a learning disability and had tested as dull normal with a Shipley intelligence quotient of 89. He had also been diagnosed as having borderline mental retardation with a mental age of nine. Raul also failed seventh grade because he was in the hospital for an extended period of time for the removal of a sewing needle that was embedded in his leg.

Raul also had a history of being sexually molested, a pattern that we discuss in Chapter 8. In Raul's case, his aunt, who had been living in the home at the time, molested the boy when he was four and five. The boy did not receive counseling for this molestation, and according to his probation officer, his mother was very defensive about the incident. According to Raul's mother, the teenager did not run with a gang, and though she worked as a nurse's aide and was gone from the house during the day, an older sister looked after the younger children. The fire Raul set caused $50,000 damage.

"Dale," age fourteen, was another typical delinquent boy. He was the second of two children and was in the ninth grade. Dale had a history of setting fires, including, at age four, setting his home bathroom on fire by placing toilet paper over an electric heater and, at age twelve, starting a kitchen fire by placing flammables over the stove. This time, he set his junior-high-school building on fire because, according to his parents, he did not want to participate in school graduation exercises. According to the police report, the boy had set two fires at school, the day after he had been "kicked out" of the house. His first fire was igniting a stack of gym clothes inside the administration building and then, a half hour later, igniting dry weeds outside the building. The boy was suspended from school.

"Claude," age sixteen, set a neighboring junior high school on fire after getting drunk at a friend's house, breaking into the school to vandalize a classroom, and then igniting the room. He said that he had been so drunk after consuming seven beers that he "didn't think right." An eleventh-grader, Claude lived with his grandparents because both his parents, who were divorced, had died the previous year. His father had committed suicide and his mother had died from a drug overdose.

Finally, "Kathy," age seventeen, was an example of a female who set a school on fire. Kathy's fire also occurred after she had been drinking, and after she had been kicked out of class for "smarting off." Kathy was in the tenth grade. Her father, who was a volunteer fire fighter, had died when she was eight, and her mother had been remarried for five years to a man Kathy disliked. According to her mother, Kathy was still troubled by her father's death.

In the interview, Kathy stated that she had previously set a telephone pole on fire when she was seven. She claimed to having smoked "pot" each day after school so that she did not have to think about her dad. She had been suspended from school the past year on four occasions for being disruptive, for drinking, for threatening a teacher, and for hitting a teacher. On the day she lit the school fire, her principal had "yelled" at her.

As we have seen, the "delinquent" firesetters are strongly influenced by their peers and share such behavioral characteristics as a disruptive home environment, emotional disturbances, sexual immaturity, aggressive or destructive behavior, and poor academic achievement. They use fire as a means of causing malicious mischief and of striking out at authority, and of covering up other crimes, such as breaking and entering. Abandoned buildings, open fields, and often schools become "fair game" to these juveniles.

Chapter Seven

"SEVERELY DISTURBED" FIRESETTERS

Bill Jones, a 14-year-old youth who lived with his mother and her alcoholic boyfriend, now has become a ward of the courts. Currently serving a one-year sentence for bringing a gun to school, Bill had been on probation for setting a Molotov cocktail through a kitchen window.

He's had a history of setting small fires as well as chaining neighborhood dogs in his backyard and abusing them. His mother, who probation workers describe as "overprotective," claims she never knew about the dogs because she never went out in the backyard.

"I used to just play with matches, and I just started setting fires," Bill explained. "I wasn't mad at nobody. I did it because I wanted to. Some people like fire, I guess, but I know I wouldn't want to get burned by one. I know the reason one guy threw cocktails was because he wanted to go to jail to get away from his father. I didn't even know why I set those fires. I wasn't doing it to be big and bad or anything like that. It just came to my mind, and I went out and did it. I did it once and I did it again. It's like I got greedy or something."[1]

The fourth category, that of "severely disturbed" firesetters, runs the gamut in age but generally constitutes a very small percentage of cases. In our San Bernardino study group, only twelve juveniles (11 percent) were categorized as severely disturbed. However, as we point out in Chapters 8 and 9, those juveniles who have been sexually abused or have sexual difficulties, and those juveniles housed in the state correctional facilities, have *all* been found by the courts to be severely disturbed and often incorrigibly delinquent.

In our small group, all but one were Caucasian and all but one were male. Most fell into the thirteen- to seventeen-year-old age category, although there were a few younger children who were quite disturbed as well. Close to 70 percent of the eighty-four items on the behavioral problems checklist typify these youngsters, according to their parents.

In general, their behavior fell into two major personality types. One type was a psychological character disorder of an "impulsive neurotic" pattern, with such characteristics as being impatient, being impulsive, stealing, destroying own possessions, and having problems sleeping. The second type was a psychological character disorder of a "borderline psychotic" pattern, with behaviors such as extreme mood swings, uncontrolled anger, violence, bizarre speech, and numerous phobias.

One of our young firesetters, "Barry," age six, fit the pattern of the "impulsive neurotic." Barry was in the first grade and was the older of two children. According to his mother, he has been in trouble since he was two and was disciplined twice a day. His father was very strict, and the boy had told his grandmother that "Daddy is mean, hates me, and gives me bad looks."

The boy's father had recently been in court for a drunk driving offense that had caused a fatality. The father was going to serve time in prison; hence, the boy was told that he would have to become the "man of the house." In response, Barry set three fires. The first was a trash fire in the kitchen; then he burned his baseball glove; finally, he set the living-room couch on fire—and that was on Father's Day. That morning, the boy had awakened before his parents, crept downstairs to the living room, set the couch on fire with matches he found lying on the counter, and then returned to his bedroom. Fortunately, smoke detectors sounded and the family was able to escape unharmed.

According to his parents, the boy turned to setting fires when he got mad at himself. In the interview, Barry said he was "dumb and stupid"—terms his parents used to describe him as well. The parents also noticed him constantly staring at the fire in the fireplace. After the last firesetting incident, the family was advised to seek psychiatric counseling for the boy.

More typical of our sample group were the teenage boys who were categorized by their probation workers and clinical psychologists as "borderline psychotic." One such juvenile was "Jason," age fourteen, the youngest of three children. Jason lived with his mother. His father was a "speed freak," a frequent user of drugs who felt that the communists were after him. His parents were divorced when Jason was one.

When Jason was ten, he was treated for borderline epilepsy. According to his mother, he could not concentrate, he could not read, and was hyperactive. A recent stressful event was the death of a close friend of his from brain cancer, a month before Jason's fire. Jason had headaches and slept day and night. He was physically immature for his age.

Jason came from a family with severe disturbances. His mother appeared hostile to society. Because of her being a prostitute over a seven-year period, the father now had legal custody of the children. However, because of the father's drug habits, the children had nearly starved while living with him. Furthermore, the boy, until the age of five, had been raised by his mother's stepmother, who had died during an abortion while Jason was at her home.

For two years prior to his fire, Jason had been out of school. Because he used profanity to a teacher, he had been expelled. His parents never bothered to reenroll him.

The boy was diagnosed as "totally incorrigible." A family of Mexicans—ethnics he disliked—lived across the street. He claimed that he had frequent fights with them and that they had "totaled his bike," a claim that was never substantiated. The reason Jason gave for his fire was that "I was sick of being beat up by Mexicans."

Having found a brochure on the Ku Klux Klan, he talked to an older neighbor who was a member of a Klan group in Orange County. In "retaliation" against this Mexican family, Jason built a cross, painted it, and stored it in his father's garage. One evening, after having words with a group of Mexicans at a Carl's Jr. fast-food restaurant, Jason set the cross up in a vacant field behind the neighbor's house, poured gasoline on it, and took off running. According to Jason, "The cross was meant for all the Mexicans to see it."

Another "borderline psychotic" in our group was "Hank," age eleven, who was deemed by his clinical psychologist to be so sociopathic that he was recommended for custodial care in a closed, structured environment. Hank's most recent offense had been eight counts of arson. His previous arrests had included two counts of burglary, petty theft, grand theft, running away from a custodial home, and trespassing.

The following detailed account, taken from the youngster's probation report, provides us with an excellent example of the "criminal careers" of these disturbed kids. Even James Cagney, as a child actor, would have been challenged by performing the role and exploits of Hank.

The boy had been beyond the control of his mother, a single parent, since he was two. His mother reported that Hank had run away from home at least fifteen times between 3½ and 5½. Well known to the Los Angeles Police Department, Hank had been picked up for "running the streets late at night in a filthy condition." Police had rescued him from rooftops and from a college swimming pool, which he had entered without permission; he was unable to swim. When disciplined by his mother, Hank would retaliate by committing malicious acts against her, including removing all the food from the refrigerator and smearing it about the walls and floors.

When the boy was five, there was an incident of arson, after which his mother decided to tie Hank, hand and foot, for safekeeping, while she was away from home. Immediately after she left, he managed to escape and proceeded to set another fire. At that time, he also threatened to set his mother on fire if she were ever to tie him up again. His threats precipitated an out-of-home placement.

After placement, at age six, the boy set a series of grass fires. In a later three-month period, he was involved in a house trailer fire, a truck fire, and an additional structural fire. Eventually placed in "Golden Acres," a residential treatment program, the boy continued to be violent, to steal, and to set fires. He was reported to be so disturbed that he could not be kept at this care facility and was therefore admitted to a hospital psychiatric unit. Reportedly, Hank's behavior grew progressively worse at this hospital, and it was decided that he should be returned to his mother's home. One reason was that he was found to be unacceptable for placement in all other treatment facilities because of his firesetting behavior.

By age eight, Hank had also been apprehended for a series of burglaries and had been placed in juvenile hall for three months. He resumed living with his mother, and the family moved to Northern California the following year. The month after this move, Hank set a grass fire. The month after that, there was a charge of petty theft and burglary. Hank had been apprehended after midnight in a post office. Two days before, he had been taken home by the police after he was reported riding alone on the city bus at 1:35 A.M.

Also at age eight, Hank and a friend stole a seventeen-foot speedboat and drove it across Lake Tahoe. When caught by police after having to stop because of engine trouble, the boy was asked where he had learned to operate such a boat and responded, "I know a lot of things for my age." He was ordered to spend 120 days in juvenile hall for this offense. Shortly after, the "Reynolds Home for Children" was recommended.

Hank did not care for this facility and felt angry at being placed so far from his mother. He and a friend ran away from the residence and stole a plane. As Hank explained the incident, they arrived at a local airport, and seeing a woman pilot about to close the door of her aircraft before taxiing down the runway, they ran up to the door of the plane and snatched her purse. When the woman got out of the plane to chase them, they circled back, got into the plane, and started down the runway themselves. Hank stated that his friend was terrified and terribly relieved when police drove onto the runway and took them into custody.

By now, the child-protective services had screened Hank for over a hundred placements with no success. Rejection was usually based on Hank's age and history of arson. Ultimately, the boy was placed in the "Garrison" home as a foster child. Mr. Garrison worked as a special-education teacher in an elementary school, and his wife worked with autistic children. They both were fully aware of Hank's troubled background.

"He created five months of misery" was how the Garrisons evaluated the nine-year-old boy's behavior while in their home. Mr. Garrison said Hank became "real nasty" and kicked Mrs. Garrison in the knees. The boy needed attention "every minute he was awake," and according to Mrs. Garrison, "it was too late for Hank."

Hank ran away from this home and was picked up by local police while riding a motorcycle he had stolen. Refusing to return to the Garrisons, whom he derided with great profanity, the boy was subsequently placed in the custody of the California Youth Authority. At eleven, Hank became one of the youngest juveniles placed in such a facility.

According to his staff psychiatrist, Hank was an ordinary-appearing adolescent. During the interview, he rearranged his chair so as to facilitate better eye-to-eye contact and smiled with delight while discussing his past behavior. He related easily to the psychiatrist and showed few signs of anxiety. Forty-five minutes into the interview, the boy cradled his head between his elbows, placed his hands behind his head, yawned frequently, played with papers on the desk, stood up, and walked around the room. For the rest of the interview, he talked about things that eleven-year-old boys usually talk about. The exception was the foul language he used. He then drummed on the desk and asked if he was about finished. At that point, the interview ended, and the boy returned to his single room in the psychiatric ward of the correctional facility.

We will have more to say about juveniles like Hank in later chapters, when we discuss the juvenile ward population of the California correctional facilities, particularly those placed since 1977. In subsequent chapters, we will also present a discussion of the treatment strategies used with these "delinquent" and "severely disturbed" firesetters.

As our case studies have demonstrated, broken homes are the common link between *all* four categories of firesetters. Broken homes have been frequently blamed as the source of delinquent behavior in general. According to a Florida study, 40 percent of children ages ten to seventeen referred to court on delinquency charges came from broken homes, but only 17 percent of children in the total population live in broken homes.[2]

In broken homes, the family members that remain are most often the mother and her children—a pattern common to our juvenile firesetters. Another study of institutionalized white boys and 500 nondelinquent boys also showed that among broken homes the most typical living arrangement for delinquent boys was the mother-only home, and that it surpassed the percentage of mother-only homes among nondelinquents.[3]

The significance of the broken home in delinquency rests in part on the functions that society expects the home to perform in rearing children. One could argue that the stigma over divorce and separation has been less acute in the lower class, where the rates are higher than in the middle class. By contrast, the psychological impact of being a "child of divorce" has been felt more heavily by children from the middle class. However, since World War II, higher divorce rates and greater tolerance of divorce have lessened the stigma for this group as well, thus, according to authorities, lessening the psychological damage to children.[4] Even so, as our study has shown, one-parent or reconstructed households appear to be the norm in the families of firesetters.

Other studies have argued that children can survive such home situations provided the relationship that they maintain with their mothers is satisfactory. The accepting, loving mother is the one with whom the child can identify and from whom he or she receives a sense of security and self-worth. The rejecting mother creates in the child a sense of resentment and unworthiness. In a study of delinquent boys, the mothers tended to be overprotective, indifferent, or, in a limited number of instances, hostile or rejecting.[5]

What these studies suggest is that children from broken homes are at greater risk than children from intact homes, but that the greater predictor of delinquent behavior is the quality of the relationship between mother and child. Thus, with our younger firesetters, the lack of proper supervision may be reflective not just of a one-parent family, where the spouse must often work for economic reasons, but of an unfavorable relationship between mother and child.

With the more severely disturbed youngsters, however, there may be other factors at work that override environmental ones. This long-standing debate is often referred to as the "nature versus nurture" controversy. Our discussion so far seems to operate under the assumption that one's social environment *is* everything, and that one-parent homes with minimal supervision result in these mixed-up kids. However, when we look at a number of examples, among which is Hank, who from a very early age did strange and unusual things, we seem to undercut that thesis and bolster the theory of the "bad seed"—or "nature"—argument. We wonder, for instance, if Hank would have been any different if his father had been at home. From what his probation officers and psychiatrists observed, we tend to doubt it. For some of these "severely disturbed" firesetters, other factors may be at work.

This debate has been fueled recently by a book on the "criminal mind," written by Stanton E. Samenow, a clinical psychologist, who contended that criminality is not caused by poverty, or neglectful parents, or indulgent ones, or "low-life" friends, or poor schools, but, instead, develops when criminals themselves make a conscious choice to be the way they are, almost from the moment they are born.[6] In a family full of conforming children, Samenow claimed, criminals are the ones who take risks, who are adventurous, and who cause trouble in school. They are the ones who provoke their parents beyond the "breaking point."

Samenow also contended that there is little that parents can do to prevent some children from gravitating toward criminal thinking and behavior:

> Even as a young child, he may have been sneaky and defiant, and the older he grew, the more he may have lied to his parents, stole and destroyed their property and threatened them. He may have made life at home unbearable as he turned even innocuous requests into declarations of war. In some cases, it is the criminal who rejects his parents rather than vice versa.[7]

One psychologist we interviewed who treats these "severely disturbed" firesetters in correctional institutions concurred that there is a "criminal mind" at work in some of them. In this regard, the category of "severely disturbed" firesetter can be distinguished from the three lesser categories of juvenile arsonists in the recognition that, for some, factors other than problem environmental conditions may be influencing their behavior. Further, the abundance and variety of behavioral problems that these serious firesetters exhibit can alert parents and authorities to the possibility of a so-called criminal mind or mentality. Moreover, as we will show in Chapter 12, the treatment process with this type of firesetter is a very complicated and lengthy one. For this reason, and because of the seriousness of their behavior and condition, the "severely disturbed" firesetters are housed in special psychiatric wards of our nation's youth training schools.

Chapter Eight

SEXUAL CONCERNS AND ARSON

Allegations that 16-year-old Mary Mirsch was sexually molested by her stepfather prior to the time she burned her handicapped brother to death last summer are under investigation, according to the San Bernardino County Sheriff's office. Mirsch, who was tried as a juvenile, has been sentenced to the California Youth Authority until she is 25 years old for murdering her 13-year-old brother, Samuel.

Dr. Lorel Wright, a child psychiatrist appointed by the court to examine the girl, said he learned she had been molested by Jason Mirsch for four years prior to the burning. He also said she told him her stepfather would threaten to beat her brother if she refused his advances. Wright said the girl appeared to be very protective of her brother, because of his physical and mental disabilities, even though she sometimes resented him. Having to submit to her stepfather in order to protect the boy and the fact other children apparently teased both of them—because of his condition—made her resentful, he explained.

Deputy Public Defender Al Smith termed Mary Mirsch a victim as well as a perpetrator and said what she did was a result of love, more than a result of malice. The stepfather was placed in custody pending the outcome of the investigation of child molestation charges.[1]

Very few females set fires as compared to males. One reason given is that parents still maintain a double standard with girls. Whereas boys are encouraged to get on their bikes and drive, girls are relegated to the backyard, where they can be supervised. Boys and girls also have different ways of orienting themselves to the world. One psychologist has argued that the higher activity level of boys, their aggressiveness, and their attempts to dominate one another all seem likely to encourage boys, more often than girls, into confrontation with adult authority both in the home and in school.[2]

Of the fires set in our San Bernardino group, 14 percent were ignited by females. This figure is somewhat high, as previous studies have found that the number of female children in their samples ranged from a low of 3 percent[3] to a high of 14 percent,[4] as in our study.

There is some indication that this pattern might be changing. One psychiatrist who has treated juvenile firesetters for many years informed us that he had recently observed greater fire play among young females who had been socialized in nontraditional ways. According to this specialist, "With the sex roles of little girls changing—such as playing with trucks rather than with dolls—girls have become more assertive and are beginning to set fires in ways similar to boys."

When questioned about the reversal of sex roles for boys and whether or not this had "decreased" their levels of fire play, the psychiatrist indicated that that had not been the case. Regardless of sex-role socialization for males, the therapist felt that boys were still continuing to play with fire. The only new trend was toward a continued increase in the frequency of girls' playing with fire.

This psychiatrist, who works in one of the intensive care units of the California Youth Authority, recounted several unusual cases involving girls and fire. One young female he treated had a habit of taking hours to scrape sulfur off matches, placing the sulfur in a pile, putting a wick in it, and then setting it on fire. Another adolescent girl, in a deliberate act of revenge, had put "trailers" (lines of sulfur or flammable material) in all parts of the house in order to burn all seven members of her family. She had been only "partially" successful, however, as the fire that she ignited harmed only three of her kin. Another teenage girl poured gasoline over her mother the day after the girl's sixteenth birthday.

These unusual accounts are borne out by other research on female firesetters. Past studies show that the female arsonist generally directs most of her firesetting against her own property, possessions, or premises. Her motives are similar to those of the males, with the exception that she seems to have more self-destructive tendencies.[5]

In a 1951 study of 201 female firesetters, the majority were found to be mentally defective, with one-third demonstrating psychosis. The older adult women were described as being lonely, unhappy, and in despair. In the adolescent females, firesetting was related to concerns about obtaining new clothes, attracting a boyfriend, or protesting against restraints.[6]

Although females who set fires are comparatively few in number, they are treated, in the words of one of the male probation officers we interviewed, "like rabid dogs." They are considered very dangerous, and authorities view firesetting by women as an extreme offense. One psychiatrist even told us, "When females do set fires, you have a real 'sicky' on your hands."

Although it is more common for girls to set fires while alone, several female juveniles in our San Bernardino group had set fires in groups. One such group was that of five fifteen-year-old females in a local high school who, smoking in the bathroom, would often deliberately set toilet paper on fire as an act of defiance against the school authorities. The arresting officer reported a suspicion of lesbian activity among the teenagers after interviewing their school counselors and principal. This lesbian behavior could not be verified.

Firesetting behavior in females has also been viewed as resulting from problems over menstruation, pregnancy, and sexually related anxieties. One investigator told us of a thirteen-year-old girl who had burned several items in her house. The fires were set exactly one month apart.

One could claim that there is a bias at work in these interpretations of female firesetting behavior. In the previous chapters, for instance, external pressures—especially divorce and broken familes—were blamed for the boys' activities. Here the girls themselves are blamed and given what could be considered trivial reasons.

Critics have long argued that the dispositions given female status offenders, for example, reflect (male) biases against females in the juvenile justice system. This argument asserts that a double standard is applied in dealing with male and female offenders. In matters of sexuality, for instance, girls are condemned and punished severely, whereas the sexuality of boys is largely ignored.[7] This double standard may affect the authorities' attitude toward female firesetters as well.

Adding "fuel to this fire," a fire chief whom we interviewed also observed that some girls set fires out of emotional fantasies of being rescued by male fire fighters because they see firemen as benevolent father figures and are infatuated with them. According to this chief, "Girls set fires to attract the firemen in much the same way some girls 'fake' a drowning in order to be rescued by the life guards." Some fire fighters, one could argue, are notoriously sexist; their walls are often covered with pornographic pictures. In this regard, they are hardly an objective source of information.

It is interesting to note that one Los Angeles fire department printed a 1984 male pin-up calendar displaying the physiques of twelve of its fire fighters. One wonders how many fire "emergencies" this calendar will elicit.

The following three cases typify the female juvenile firesetters in our study group.

"Julie," age nine, began setting fires soon after her parents divorced when she was seven. An only child, Julie was considered physically immature for her age. According to her mother, Julie was disciplined at least once a week. Her most recent fire was setting the grass and leaves on fire in her backyard. Julie told her psychologist that she often dreamed about fire at night and that, in these dreams, "the house has burned up."

With "Elizabeth," age thirteen, the fire seemed to be set as an act of revenge. Elizabeth was in the eighth grade. Though her parents were divorced when she was six years old, she continued to visit her father on weekends. Elizabeth's fire was regarded by fire officials as extremely serious. Planning her fire for two weeks, she said, "I thought it would be easy." Her intentions were to kill her siblings, her mother, and her stepfather. She took a school paper and set the bathroom and the curtain in one sister's bedroom on fire. When later asked why she started the fire, she explained, "I wished them dead." Recounting her daydreams about fire to her psychologist, Elizabeth said, "I picture the whole house on fire. Everyone in the house gets out except for me."

Elizabeth felt that her parents were "nice to other people but yell and scream at me." She stated that her older sister hit her, her younger sister yelled at her, and her brother teased her. She also stated that her mother fought with her stepfather. Recently, Elizabeth had gone to live with her father for a month, but conditions had not im-

proved as she always had to babysit for the children of her
father and his second wife and clean the kitchen. Contem-
plating running away from her father's home, Elizabeth
decided against it out of fear of what might happen to her
alone on the street. Instead, she decided to burn her mother's house down.

Another troubled, revengeful, female juvenile firesetter was "Jill." Like the other girls, this ten-year-old, an
only child, came from a divorced family. Further, within
the six months prior to her most recent fire, Jill and her
family had moved three times. All five of Jill's fires were
serious. She was brought to the attention of authorities for
lighting her mother's bedroom carpet. Before this, Jill had
ignited her mother's bedspread and bedsheets while her
mother's boyfriend, a man she obviously disliked, was in
the adjoining bathroom taking a shower. Unable to control
her daughter, Jill's mother brought her to the San Bernardino probation department's fire-safety program for
counseling.

At least one-third of the girls in our sample group had
been victims of sexual abuse, which accounted for their
firesetting behavior. Further, we suspect that many more
of the other girls had also been sexually molested but
didn't admit to it for fear of possible reprisal from the offending parent, embarrassment over the incident, or a
tendency to blame themselves for having been victimized.

Research into child sexual abuse has indicated that
adults (and older siblings) who engage in such behavior
with underage children tend to do so out of a need for
power and control rather than for sexual satisfaction or
release.[8] Regardless of the motive, such abuse generates
incalculable psychological problems for the victim, as the
following cases from our group of juvenile firesetters
show.

"Amy," age fourteen, was sexually victimized by her natural father. Apprehended for lighting a brushfire, Amy came from a family that had all the warning signs of an "incest family." Her mother was overbearing, insisting that Amy perform all of the household chores because the mother was recuperating from a lengthy illness. Her father was a severe alcoholic and abusive to both his wife and his children. The sexual incidents occurred when the mother was either sick in a separate bedroom in the house or when she was hospitalized.

"Terri," age thirteen, also set a brushfire. Terri was first abused at age five, when she was sexually fondled by an in-law family member. The effects of this early abuse persisted for many years in her depressive moods. Because of health problems that were psychologically generated, she had had to take medication for several years. When she was seven, she had to have her stomach pumped because of overmedication. Terri's parents were divorced when she was six, and Terri had been living with her mother and her mother's third husband. According to her mother, Terri suffered from numerous physical ailments, including stomachaches and convulsions. She also had sleeping problems and nightmares and was scared of men.

"Mary," age thirteen, had also been sexually abused. Like the others, Mary's parents were divorced. Mary had been molested by her stepfather. In addition, Mary suffered from dyslexia and had been placed in special-education classes. The kids at school teased her, and she often dreamed about fire as a way of getting back at them. Mary set a fire at school, and her mother's response, on hearing of the charges brought against her daughter, was a demand to know what discipline she should take in reprimanding the girl. In a remark indicative of the lack of a quality home life, this mother—who knew of the child's earlier sexual molestation—told the arresting officer,

"Mary has been raked over the coals thoroughly, but the only kind of punishment that is going to do any good is the kind that hurts enough to make the child fear misbehavior because of associating it with pain."

It is typical of these incestuous home situations that the girls are blamed for behavior that has been perpetrated against them. As past research has shown, most mothers of female incest victims are married to men who have unrealistic expectations of them. Unable to comply with these men's demands, they either force their daughter(s) to fulfill the demands, or they resort to illness or withdrawal, leaving their daughter(s) vulnerable to the sexual demands of the dominant male figure in the home. These adolescent girls, therefore, who become incest victims, have been cast in the role of a "surrogate" mother or wife.[9]

The incestuous family is obviously a pathological system. The individual family member caught in this web has great difficulty extricating herself or himself from the nightmare. As one psychologist told us, "With parents who are rigid and domineering, some kids will roll over and be submissive little soldiers. Others will fight it and run away." And others, as our study shows, resort to setting fires.

Child sexual abuse is not limited to females. As we mentioned in the last chapter, one of the male juveniles in our San Bernardino sample group had been sexually molested by an aunt when he was a young child. No other male juvenile in our study group, however, appeared to have been sexually victimized. However, a discussion of such occurrences does not often take place with boys. Probation officers and social workers are much more apt to suspect sexual abuse with female offenders, but questions concerning sexual abuse are not often asked of male juveniles. Despite our interest in this topic, not all of the males in our group were asked questions concerning the possibility of such abuse, as some fire-safety personnel felt uncomfortable raising the issue. Furthermore, the government's classification manual does not include sexual abuse as a behavioral problem, and so the parents are not asked about this issue either.

To shed more light on the topic of the sexual abuse of boys we quote here from a psychiatrist who treats "severely disturbed" firesetters in correctional institutions. (We will return to other aspects of this interview in Chapter 12.)

Q: Have you treated any juvenile male firesetters who were sexually molested?

A: Several. One boy I worked with progressed from setting fires to fields, to shooting birds, to hanging cats, to blowing his father's head off with a shotgun. He started setting fires when he was young, after an incident in which an older brother who had just had a motorcycle accident had died in his sleep. This brother had sexually molested him when he was eleven.

Q: Any other cases?

A: Another boy at age ten had tried to kill his cousin by putting poison in his Kool Aid. He was released from juvenile hall at eleven, and we knew he would become a repeat offender, but there was nothing we could do as the courts had mandated his release. At twenty-two, he was again apprehended and confessed that he had killed four kids.

As a nine-year-old youngster he had been repeatedly raped by his uncle and his uncle's friends over a four-year period. When he began to kill, he first murdered an adolescent boy. His later three victims were boys six to nine years of age. He would pick the kids up, feed them, have sex with them, and then strangle them. His original damage to the world had been setting fires.

Q: What accounts for this intense rage?

A: Boys such as these who have been sexually "violated" harbor an enormous amount of rage. Their fantasies of violent rage are even more severe if the boys have been anally penetrated rather than orally copulated. Firesetting becomes for these boys the means of total eradication of the offending object. Criminal offenders who have been sexually exploited almost always link their firesetting with their sexual abuse.

We would concur with these observations. Both boys and girls who have been sexually victimized are at greater risk than other children. And without proper and early intervention, their anger at being sexually victimized can lead to very serious criminal acts.

For other juveniles, the firesetting behavior stems not only from incest but from other sexually related issues and anxieties. The case of "Tammy," age fifteen, for example, shows how a juvenile, in rebelling against too strict a fundamentalist church upbringing, may act out in sexually inappropriate ways. According to her probation officer, Tammy grew up with rigid parental and religious codes. She rebelled against their tight stricture but still maintained a fear that for her actions, she was going to "burn in hell."

Tammy appeared to have set her family's house on fire as a means of "crying for help" because of a sexual situation that she could not handle. Her own dog died in the fire. She was five months pregnant at the time of her fire, and her psychological tests right after the fire indicated that she was very confused and extremely emotionally insecure. According to her clinical psychologist, in her sexual relationship, Tammy sought out a substitute father figure who would dominate her, as the following detailed psychological evaluation indicates:

> The underlying, initial dynamics appear to stem from conflicts in the father–daughter sphere. Tammy's immaturity and feelings of insecurity derived from a need to be

domineered by a father figure. Her need to be dominated was met outside her relationship with her natural father. Tammy became very dependent and passive-submissive in her substitute domineering father-figure relationship. Therefore, the onset of a sexual relationship with this father figure brought into emotional play the characteristics common to victims of incest *and* the hostility that sexually exploited children and adolescents experience.

Her fear of losing the security she had in the relationship increased her passive-submissive manner and her need to close out any awareness of the inappropriateness of the relationship. The emotional conflicts were further compounded when she was requested to commit antisocial acts (stealing) in addition to sexual submission. Each new involvement and commitment to the relationship required an equal increase in her defenses against awareness.

It is important to note that she completely denied an awareness of her pregnancy until the relationship was terminated and she was detained at juvenile hall. The only apparent breakthrough in her defense system was an awareness that she had deliberately killed her dog when she set fire to the house. The death of the dog appeared to provide her an avenue in which she could safely express her emotionality without fear of being flooded with a full awareness of her distressful situation. Regarding her pregnancy, she simply denied its existence, hoping it would "just go away."

In one study of female arsonists in a psychiatric population, it was found that they generally had more problems related to sexuality than did a control group of female nonarsonists. The arsonists were more likely to be considerably active sexually than the controls, and they reported having their first sexual experience at a younger age (fifteen) than did female nonarsonists (twenty).[10]

By contrast, male arsonists showed lower rates of sexual activity than nonarsonists, at least in psychiatric populations. Even so, firesetting has often been considered a sexually motivated activity, especially in males. In a 1955 study, it was observed that male firesetters had engaged in such behavior as exhibiting their genitals, looking under women's skirts, and mutual masturbation and fellatio. Such behavior was interpreted as reflecting the direct expression of infantile sexual and aggressive behavior, including voyeurism and exhibitionism.[11]

The case of "Edgar," age fourteen, documents some of these patterns of the sexually acting-out male firesetter. Edgar grew up in an upper-middle-class home with his father, his stepmother, and a step-sister his own age. He was a straight "A" student who excelled in sports.

The precipitating event that brought him to juvenile hall was the incident of his stealing acid from a chemistry lab at school and placing it in the bus seat where a girl, who had refused him a date, usually sat. Edgar was assigned to a San Bernardino County probation officer who worked with firesetters because he had previously set numerous fires when he was a preadolescent, ages eight to eleven.

In an interview with the stepmother, she mentioned that she had found several graphic pictures that the boy had drawn. In some of these pictures, men were displayed with exaggerated sex organs in erection, and in others, there were scenes with knives, daggers, and lightning bolts. She had also found knives under his pillow on several occasions. The probation officer felt that the knives very likely represented a sexual fetish to the boy and that he was possibly using them to masturbate with.

The boy had lived with this family for the past 1½ years. Before that, he had lived with his natural mother and visited his father during summer vacation. His natural mother mentioned that when Edgar was eleven, she had entered his bedroom to find him whipping his own dog, which he had bound and gagged. When confronted with this behavior, the boy began to cry, became uncommunicative, and could give no explanation for what he had done. His mother had also found female sex magazines in his room. On one nude model, Edgar had drawn a tattoo that said "mother."

Earlier accounts of cases like Edgar referred to these male juveniles as "sex 'pyros.'" Accordingly, sex pyros set fires to achieve sexual stimulation and orgasm. For these youngsters, arson is used as a substitute for sexual acts, and these arsonists derive a sexual thrill from setting a fire and watching the flames.[12]

In our study, one male, "William," age seventeen, fit the description of a sexually confused firesetter. He was currently being treated by the California Youth Authority after being apprehended for setting a series of major forest fires and brushfires. The second of two boys, William was tall and gangling in appearance, shy and somewhat awkward. His parents, according to the juvenile, were "extremely strict and demanding." When family pressure became too intense, William would merely get on his bike and ride off in "any which direction." Often, when he would stop, he would masturbate to relieve the tension. Soon another pattern developed. At the point where he would stop, he would light a fire. In this case, William developed a stimulus–response linking sexual masturbation with lighting fires as a means of releasing the tension and anger he felt toward his parents.

Masturbation, it appears, is used by these youngsters in one of two ways. Either they masturbate as a defense against the setting of fires, or the excitement generated by the fires they set stimulates them sexually to the point of masturbation. In William's case, both patterns were present. A compulsive masturbator, William reported that he had engaged in this form of sexual release at least ten times a day since he was fifteen years old.

It is interesting to note that, in the behavioral characteristics portion of our study, we asked the parents of both our firesetters and our controls whether or not their child masturbated. We fully expected that there would be significant differences between the two groups. No differences were found, however. The vast majority of parents in both groups indicated that their offspring *never* masturbated (92 percent of firesetters and 84 percent of nonfiresetters), with the remaining percentages referring to their offspring as only *sometimes* masturbating. No parents in either group reported that their child *frequently* masturbated. And these findings held even when the age of the juvenile was taken into consideration. In effect, this response indicates that the parents very likely knew little about the masturbatory behavior of their offspring— granted, a private act—because frequent masturbation was admitted by at least some of the teenage male firesetters.

In a similar vein, the parents were also asked to indicate, on the list of behavioral characteristics, whether or not their child had been sexually active with others. Once again no differences were noted between the two study groups. Both sets of parents perceived their offspring as *not* being sexually active.

Earlier in the book, we cautioned the reader about basing knowledge of juvenile firesetters solely on the parents' perceptions of their offspring's behavior. But as our study has shown, by analyzing the case studies, by observing the firesetters themselves, by discussing our findings with treatment personnel and the like, and by documenting our findings with those of earlier research, we *have* been able to explain and clarify the patterns of behavior that the parents of firesetters in our San Bernardino group observed with their children.

Matters concerning sexuality need further clarification, however, as the parents' perceptions in this area are inconsistent with the juveniles' actual behavior. Parents' awareness of masturbation and sexual activity among their children is often limited, as the parents are not likely to be present when the activity is taking place, and because sexual issues involving juveniles are not generally discussed (or admitted to) among family members in our society.

Previous research has argued that there is a connection between (latent) homosexuality and arson. One study in 1951, for example, revealed numerous case histories in which a "confused" sex life—meaning being "passive participants in homosexual play"—contributed to firesetting.[13] Likewise, another early study in 1954 claimed that difficulties in developing a "normal" heterosexual relationship out of shyness, partial impotence, or fear of acquiring a venereal infection might lead young boys to homosexual experimentation. Such individuals, it was claimed, would not therefore develop "normal inhibitions" against such "sexual maladjustments" and, therefore, would be more prone to engage in antisocial acts such as firesetting.[14] This view implies that homosexual experimentation can lead to fire play.

In understanding this pattern—if, in fact, it exists—we must be careful to distinguish between teenage homosexual activity or sex play and an adult sexual orientation toward homosexuality.

None of the male juveniles in our San Bernardino group were identified by their psychologists, probation officers, or parents as being homosexual. Nor did any of the youngsters voluntarily self-report a homosexual identity. The specific question of whether or not they identified themselves as homosexual was not asked, however. As with the questions concerning masturbation and sexual activity, the parents of our San Bernardino group of firesetters did not disclose their offspring's sexual orientation. (Furthermore, the question concerning sexual orientation is not included in the government's classification manual.) But as we mentioned earlier, a group of females had been suspected of lesbian activity. And several gay juvenile firesetters were part of the state correctional institution population.

Future research is needed to clarify in what ways the self-defined homosexual adolescent may or may not differ from the self-defined heterosexual adolescent with respect to all forms of delinquent behavior, including firesetting. Homosexual adolescents have been found to be more meek in demeanor and more passive-aggressive than non-homosexual adolescents.[15] But this psychological profile, common to our juvenile firesetters as well, does not imply a correlation between a homosexual identity and an involvement with arson.

According to the correctional institution psychiatrist we interviewed, firesetting behavior develops when children are young, before they have dealt with their sexuality and have developed sexual patterns. Although not ruling out a later same-sex orientation, this psychiatrist contended that arson and sexual orientation are two independent variables. In other words, one activity does not necessarily lead to the other.

Because none of the male juveniles in our San Bernardino group were self-reportedly homosexual, we interviewed a gay adult male who had been a firesetter as a youngster. In his startlingly candid account, he noted that fantasies and activities of firesetting were replaced by those of sexuality, including masturbation and homosexual activity:

> I was a firestarter up to the age of twelve. But I don't know how to apply the fact that I was a firestarter to where I am now as an adult. One of the things I can say for sure is that the firestarting eventually took second place to sex as I entered puberty, and that I became cautious and scared when I was around nine years old when I almost burned our house down. I lit the toilet paper roll in the bathroom. The affair was known only to me. I quickly put the fire out and cleaned up the room. But I was almost overcome by all the smoke, and it frightened the living daylights out of me. From that point on, I stayed away from large fires. But the fascination was still there.
>
> When I was twelve years old, a friend my age almost started an empty field on fire. The flames got out of hand, but he was able to get hold of them and put the fire out. Although I didn't see the fire, he told me about it right after the incident. I remember we were at his house, and I was afraid for him and appalled and fascinated at the same time. I remember being very aware that I had outgrown that kind of thing, but what amazed me was that this friend waited till his mother came home and proceeded to tell her. Now, he didn't have to tell her—she wouldn't have known otherwise. She became extremely angry and started screaming. She kicked me out of the house—there wasn't a father in the family. The next day, he told me he received a spanking. This friend was also extremely sexual. But I was cautious of him because he had a tendency to tell all, and I soon dropped him as a friend.
>
> I don't know how many fires I've started. But there were a lot of them—mostly small—in an ashtray, in the toilet bowl (this was my favorite place), lighting up a whole book of matches, starting my model cars on fire—nothing big or important. For me, it all started with lighting my mother's cigarettes. It became an obsession for me and I especially remember my mother being very amused and

almost encouraging. I was the one that always had to light the barbecue, the fireworks, and so on. Like I said, these were exciting and obsessive.

I have never related my sexual activity with the fact that I was a firestarter. The only comparison I can make is with masturbation. My firestarting was a small, private affair, always alone. I was never with friends, unlike masturbation and sex, where I was always seeking friends. The similar feelings during the fires were eventually replaced with masturbation. I had always masturbated. With the onset of puberty, self-abuse suddenly became exciting. Although I couldn't always find a partner, masturbation, like firestarting, became extremely private. Even with a partner, sex was extremely private. My friends from that point on were almost always selected with sexual participation in mind. All of my friends became sexual partners in some way or another, or they weren't my friends.

Like masturbation, firestarting was an act of comfort that allowed me to have my private fantasies. But firestarting was more dreamlike, and wishing I were somewhere else. When I was very young the fantasies were of Superman, Flash Gordon, and other hero figures. What I'm trying to say is that the hypnotizing effect of the fire allowed me to drift and think and wish and dream. I was and still am a person with strong fantasies.

We have shown a link in this chapter between sexual concerns and arson. Though female firesetters are less common, they are often viewed as more serious offenders than male firesetters because deviant behavior in females is less socially acceptable. Furthermore, at least one-third of the female juveniles in our San Bernardino group had been victims of sexual assault, a situation that greatly influenced their delinquent behavior. Likewise, male juvenile firesetters in correctional institutions have been observed to have been sexually victimized. Finally, for some male juveniles, arson is linked with sexual behavior, including masturbation, sexual fantasies, and homosexual activity. No direct correlation has been found, however, between arson and a gay or lesbian orientation.

Chapter Nine

JUVENILE ARSONISTS IN PRISON

David Berkowitz, the confessed "Son of Sam" mass murderer who terrorized New York City during 1976 and 1977 by killing five young women and a man and wounding seven other young people, also reportedly informed his attorneys that he set over 2,000 fires and made 337 false alarms in New York City from 1974 through 1977. On almost every occasion, he reportedly called in the fires to the police as the "Phantom of the Bronx."

According to a newspaper account, Berkowitz claimed that he set these fires in cars, rubbish, brush and vacant and unoccupied stores. Allegedly, he set 11 of these fires on a single day and two less than a month prior to his last killing just a block away from the future murder site.

The newspaper further reported that childhood friends of Berkowitz recalled that Berkowitz—who dreamed of becoming a fire fighter—had a car outfitted with a fire radio and that he would sit in the "navigator's" seat and log the blazes in detail.

Note-pads seized by the authorities, allegedly bearing the handprinted notes of Berkowitz, gave detailed information of 1,411 fires for the years of 1974, 1975, and 1977, including the date and time of the fire, street, borough, weather, number of the fire box, and the fire department code indicating the type of responding apparatus and building or property burned.[1]

At age four, Steven Jones set an empty doghouse on fire. At six, his father gave him a beating for setting a mat-

113

tress on fire in his grandmother's garage. "I did those fires just for the fun of it," Jones recalls.

Today, at sixteen, he's serving a year-and-a-half sentence in one of the California Youth Authority institutions. His offense? Burning out two rooms in his foster parents' home. "There was really no reason why I did it," Jones says. "It was just something that came to my mind. I just did it." Asked if he was angry when he threw the lighter fluid in the bedroom and on the living room carpet, he replied, "I was mad, yeah, 'cause I couldn't go home. I wanted to go home."

A poor student in school, largely because of his truancy, he speaks in barely audible mumbles. "My father and me didn't get along so well," he says. "Since I was locked up, we been talking more. That was always the problem—him and me."[2]

The more serious cases of young arsonists are handled through the juvenile courts, and these arsonists are usually sentenced to state penal and medical institutions. These more serious offenders, who were not part of our sample San Bernardino group, are the subject of this chapter.

We will begin by:

1. Analyzing data of 192 cases provided us from the research division of the California Youth Authority (CYA) on all juvenile arsonists sentenced in California between the years 1977 and 1982
2. Noting the procedures by which a juvenile is sentenced to the CYA
3. Comparing the profile of a "typical" CYA male and a "typical" female ward with that of a "typical" CYA juvenile arsonist
4. Presenting interviews that we conducted with a wide range of professionals who work with these troubled firesetters in the correctional facility setting

In order for juvenile arson and firesetting to come under juvenile court jurisdiction, the offender must be under age eighteen at the time of commission. If the youngster is under age fourteen, there must be clear proof that, at the time of offense, the individual knew its wrongfulness. Specifically, the law states that she or he "must appreciate the intrinsic and moral wrongfulness of the act itself, not just knowledge that there might be consequences."

As we discussed in Chapter 2, the penal code further defines arson or other unlawful burning of property as including the requirement of the acts being "willful and malicious" or "willful with the intent to defraud." By contrast, a small child who, while playing with matches, accidentally sets a building afire is negligent but is not guilty of arson. Cases such as these are handled civilly, without the intervention of the criminal or juvenile justice system.

In the case of a minor under age eighteen believed involved in a crime, he or she eventually appears before a judge at a proceeding known as an *adjudication*. According to the district attorney's office, the word *punishment* may not be used, only the word *rehabilitation*, as the emphasis is on assisting these juveniles to develop appropriate social behavior. There is talk, however, in the California legislature, and elsewhere in the country, of making some of the treatment of these juvenile crimes that of punishment.

If the juvenile is found guilty, one of five actions may be taken, in increasing levels of severity. The juvenile may simply be sent to his or her own home on probation. If the court feels that he or she is not receiving proper supervision at home, the juvenile may be placed in a suitable foster home or in a residential care facility. More serious or recidivist offenders may be sent to a county camp and placed on a work detail (including fighting forest fires).

Finally, juvenile offenders may be sent to a closed institution under the auspices of the California Youth Authority, generally until age twenty-one, at which time they are set free. In certain aggravated cases involving a juvenile under age eighteen, he or she may be tried as an adult if it can be shown in judicial proceedings that he or she cannot be rehabilitated.

Several criminological studies have been conducted that compare the patterns and the psychological profiles of juvenile and adult criminals. Some of these studies include comparing and contrasting the arson offender with other types of felony offenders, as well as differentiating between types of arson offenders.

One arson investigator for a fire department in Los Angeles County claimed that each firesetter, like other ritualistic-style criminals, leaves evidence of his or her personality at the fire scene. This is particularly true of the older, more seriously disturbed firesetter. Whereas the younger (eleven- to fourteen-year-old) juveniles tend to set fires in groups, the recidivist firesetter returns alone to the same area—his or her "fire turf"—and sets fire to it several times. This investigator recounted how he had been able to apprehend a juvenile who had set a series of costly brushfires using a common "cigarette–matchbook method," whereby a lighted cigarette is inserted in a matchbook to act as a time fuse that ignites the match heads. He recalled:

> Last autumn we apprehended a youth who had been using the procedure. He aroused our suspicions because he seemed to be always at the scene when the firemen arrived. And he often had descriptions of people he said he had seen setting the blazes. We staked him out and eventually caught him in the act.[3]

Similarities have been noted among kids who kill their parents, using any number of means including shooting, stabbing, bludgeoning, choking, or poisoning them, as well as burning them to death. Children who engage in parricide have often tried other outs to extricate themselves from their circumstances before committing the fatal acts. They have asked relatives or school counselors for assistance, or they have attempted to run away from home. Unfortunately, the authorities they ask to intervene on their behalf may just assure the child that everything will be all right. Often a child who is thinking of killing a parent has told some other person about what he or she is intending to do.[4]

Athough all children who engage in serious offenses share many environmental and psychological characteristics, firesetters, by contrast, are often more physically and emotionally weak. This weakness may cause them to avoid personal confrontations with people they dislike and thus may lead them instead to fire. According to this point of view, fire is considered a passive-aggressive act in that it allows the arsonist to assert his or her own superiority in one grand gesture.

Another important distinction between arsonists and other criminals is the highly symbolic and complex nature of the arson act. The severely disturbed arsonist engages in what has been referred to as a *firesetting syndrome*. This syndrome includes

> turning in the alarm, waiting for the firemen to arrive, watching and assisting in the extinguishing operation, establishing a relationship with firemen, using the firesetting as a signal to obtain help, and expressing intense sexual excitement and destructive wishes and impulses through the firesetting behavior.[5]

Other types of felony offenses, excluding homicide, are thought *not* to be this complex and symbolic.

Another study noted the similarities between arsonists and sex offenders in terms of the reaction they elicit from the community at large, as well as from justice and law-enforcement agencies.[6] In fact, one could argue that the public is even more horrified by arsonists because of the scope of the consequences of their crime, the widespread destruction that a fire can bring about. The sex offender, on the other hand, is rarely a menace to as great a number of people.

Common behavioral characteristics have also been noted in a study of prisoners who have committed a variety of aggressive crimes. Over two-thirds (70 percent) of these violent felons had set fires as children, had been bedwetters, and had been cruel to animals. Nearly all of them (95 percent) had had a history of parental loss.[7]

The California Youth Authority handles only the more serious delinquent and disturbed juvenile arsonists. For example, of 995 juvenile arsonists arrested in the State of California in 1981, the CYA received forty-four (4 percent) of them. Only 1 percent of the total Youth Authority commitments for 1981, moreover, were for arson offenses (44 out of a total of 4,083). All but 2 of these 44 juveniles were male.

Both the percentage and the total number of arsonists to be committed to the Youth Authority, however, have increased in the ten-year period from 1971 to 1981. (These figures are noted in Table B-18.) Whereas the number of arsonists in 1971 ($N = 24$) represented 0.7 percent of the total population committed, their percentage steadily increased to 0.8 percent in 1976 ($N = 29$), and to a 1.1 percent total in 1981 ($N = 44$). It should be pointed out, however, as Table B-18 also indicates, that arson was only one of several offenses that showed such an increase. Both offenses against persons, such as homicide and rape, and offenses against property, such as burglary and theft, showed similar increases.

Before discussing the profile of the "typical" arsonist consigned to the Youth Authority, we will examine, for comparative purposes, the composite profile of the "typical" male and female wards under the auspices of the same authority who are in correctional institutions for *all* crimes.

Based on material collected for the 1981 annual report of the Department of the Youth Authority for the State of California, typical *male* juveniles shared the following characteristics: they came from neighborhoods that were below average economically (46 percent), from average neighborhoods (48 percent), or from above-average neighborhoods (6 percent). One-third (35 percent) lived in neighborhoods with a high level of delinquency compared to only a few (7 percent) who lived in neighborhoods considered nondelinquent. One-third (35 percent) came from homes where all or part of the family income came from public assistance.

With respect to family background, only 29 percent came from unbroken homes. One natural parent was present in an additional 62 percent of the homes. Furthermore, over half of the male wards had at least one other family member—either a parent or a sibling—who had a delinquent or criminal record.

As for delinquent behavior, the major problem for these males was undesirable peer influence (44 percent). With regard to schooling, 21 percent of the male wards were last enrolled in the ninth grade or below, and only 19 percent had reached the twelfth grade or had graduated from high school.

The profile of the CYA *female* in correctional institutions for all crimes varies to some degree from that of the male. In terms of home environment, 41 percent of the females came from neighborhoods that were below average economically, 49 percent came from average neighborhoods, and 10 percent came from above-average neighborhoods. Similar to the male, one-third of the females (33 percent) lived in neighborhoods with a high level of delinquency. Only 9 percent lived in neighborhoods considered nondelinquent.

With respect to family background, a slightly smaller percentage of females came from unbroken homes (24 percent). But like the males, over half of the female wards had at least one parent or sibling who had a delinquent or criminal record. As to schooling, one-third of the females were last enrolled in the ninth grade or below, and only 18 percent had reached the twelfth grade or had graduated from high school.

The major difference between the sexes was their problem areas as determined by the correctional facility psychologists. Whereas males were more likely to be diagnosed as having become delinquent because of undesirable peer influences, the major problem areas diagnosed for females were mental and emotional problems (37 percent). But as we pointed out in Chapter 8, there may be some sexual bias at work in these diagnoses, as females are disproportionately blamed for internal problems, males for external ones.

For comparative purposes, we requested and received, from the research division of the California Youth Authority, background information on the 192 juvenile arsonists under their jurisdiction during the five-year period between 1977 and 1982. A discussion of these background characteristics and patterns will enable us to draw a clearer picture of the "typical" juvenile arsonist who is regarded by the state as a serious offender. This profile will then be compared with that of the typical CYA male and female wards incarcerated for a variety of offenses.

Of these 192 recently incarcerated young arsonists, 95 percent (183) were males, and 61 percent were Caucasian, followed by 21 percent Hispanic, 12 percent black, and 6 percent other.

The range in age at the time they were incarcerated was from eleven to twenty-four. The reasons that some young adults were placed in the CYA facilities were that they were first offenders and the courts felt that they could benefit from the special rehabilitative programs offered by the Youth Authority. By contrast, as adults in adult prisons under the jurisdiction of the Department of Corrections, there would be minimal emphasis on rehabilitation. Further, those juvenile arsonists who are under age eleven are placed in diversion programs or foster-care facilities and are *not* sent to the closed Youth Authority institutions. This fact accounts for the median age of the juvenile arsonists, which is somewhat older than seventeen.

For statistical purposes, we grouped their ages into three categories: the young juveniles (ages eleven to sixteen; $N = 69$); the older juveniles (ages seventeen and eighteen; $N = 70$); and the young adults (nineteen to twenty-four; $N = 53$).

With respect to prior record, the juvenile arsonists' profile included the following: those with no prior record for arson or any crime (21 percent); those with some prior petitions or writeups (28 percent); those with one prior record (27 percent); and those with more than one prior record (24 percent). For arson, it appears that those with no prior record were just as likely to be incarcerated as those with a record of police arrests.

The home life of these incarcerated arsonists also varied. In terms of parental figures in the home, one-fourth (26 percent) lived with both natural parents, 30 percent lived with either their natural mother or their natural father, and 26 percent lived in some other type of family arrangement; unfortunately, we have no information available for the remaining 18 percent.

Most of the arsonists came from families that received no public assistance (58 percent), and others received some public assistance (18 percent). No information was available for 24 percent. One-fourth of the juveniles came from below-average economic neighborhoods (27 percent), and in direct contrast to the typical CYA ward, nearly half (49 percent) came from average neighborhoods or from above-average neighborhoods (4 percent). For some (20 percent), the economic aspect of the neighborhood was not reported.

Delinquency in their neighborhoods followed similar patterns. Some juvenile arsonists came from high-delinquency neighborhoods (16 percent); others came from moderately delinquent areas (35 percent); and others came from non- or low-delinquency areas (30 percent), a direct contrast to the typical CYA ward. For some 19 percent of arsonists, the delinquency of the neighborhood was not reported.

The major adjustment problems, as determined by the correctional facility clinical psychologists in the reception centers, also varied for these firesetters. Although these seem like facile distinctions as one category slips into the other, adjustment problems were differentiated. Those with mental and emotional problems accounted for the highest percentage (35 percent). They were followed by those with negative peer influence (23 percent) and those with family conflicts (10 percent). The remaining major adjustment problems were either job-related, drug-related, or school-related problems (12 percent). Major adjustment problems were not reported for some juveniles (20 percent).

A *psychological profile* was also established for each of the arsonists. The California Youth Authority employs a classification system based on *maturity type*.[8] The system is rooted in a theory that assumes a developmental explanation for human behavior. Arguing that personalities mature in stages similar to those of physical maturing, the theory postulates that delinquency occurs when there is a failure by the individual to develop the appropriate skills in a given stage. This failure leads to serious problems in adjusting to interpersonal relationships.

In this schema, there are three broad levels of interpersonal maturity for individuals that are relevant to delinquency. The first category, the *unsocialized delinquents*, includes those individuals who are the most serious offenders, relating to their environment in the most primitive way, and forming very few emotional ties with others. Relating to others as if they were objects, they are unable to accurately gauge other people's reactions to them and to adjust themselves accordingly. They also have minimal self-control and are unable to plan for the future. They respond to their predicament in one of two extreme ways: either by aggressively confronting their environment or, conversely, by passively adapting to it as best they can.

The second category, the *conformist delinquents*, includes those who related very superficially to those around them but who have gained enough insight into human behavior to develop a strategy that attempts to gain their ends by winning approval from those whom they most respect or whom they perceive as wielding power. In this fashion, those above them in the hierarchy are manipulated and those beneath them are coerced into satisfying their own egocentric needs.

Finally, in the third category, the *neurotic delinquents* have a greater interpersonal maturity than the first two levels in that they have developed some social skills, can form bonds of affection, and can regulate their behavior to take into consideration the needs of others. Neverthe-less, the neurotics exhibit overwhelming feelings of un-worthiness and guilt; they are easily discouraged in their attempts to improve themselves; and they remain vulner-able to exploitation by other people. The neurotics, how-ever, respond more favorably to therapy than do the more serious unsocialized and conformist groups because they have developed the capacity for learning and adopting so-cial skills.[9]

Of the 192 juvenile arsonists in prison, more were di-agnosed by prison psychologists as having psychological profiles as conformists (37 percent)—the second level of severity—than as either neurotics (31 percent) or as the more serious unsocialized offenders (8 percent). A psy-chological profile was not measured for some wards, how-ever (24 percent).

In conclusion, when comparing the profile of the "typical" juvenile arsonist with that of the composite of the "typical" juvenile ward, one clear distinction emerges. The arsonists generally came from higher socioeconomic backgrounds in that they were *less* likely to come from economically impoverished neighborhoods, areas with high rates of juvenile delinquency, and families that re-ceived public assistance. In other background areas, how-ever, the juvenile arsonists shared a number of character-istics with the typical CYA ward, such as home life, parents' marital status, and major adjustment problem areas.

Using the raw data provided us from the Youth Au-thority on these 192 juvenile arsonists, we uncovered sev-eral statistically significant patterns:

1. Caucasians were much more likely to be diagnosed as neurotics (the less severe category), and blacks

and Hispanics were much more likely to be diagnosed as conformists. As Table B-19 shows, over half of the whites (53 percent) were diagnosed as neurotics compared with only 16 percent of the blacks and 21 percent of the Hispanics. By contrast, three-quarters of the blacks were diagnosed as conformists (78 percent) compared to two-thirds of the Hispanics (65 percent) and one-third of the whites (35 percent). Further, whites (11 percent) and Hispanics (14 percent) were twice as likely to be diagnosed as the more serious unsocialized as were blacks (6 percent).

2. Close to half the whites (49 percent) came from neighborhoods where delinquency was either low in rate or nonexistent. By contrast, half the Hispanics (52 percent) came from moderately delinquent neighborhoods, and over half the blacks came from neighborhoods with high delinquency rates.

3. Similarly, the white arsonists were more likely to come from neighborhoods with either an average or an above-average standard of living as compared to Hispanics and blacks, who came from areas of an average or a below-average standard of living. Whereas only one-fourth of the whites (25 percent) came from economically deprived neighborhoods, one-third of the blacks (36 percent) and nearly two-thirds of the Hispanics (63 percent) came from impoverished communities.

4. In terms of adjustment problems, whites were diagnosed more often as having mental and emotional problems (46 percent) than were blacks (35 percent) and Hispanics (22 percent). By contrast, Hispanics and blacks were more frequently diagnosed as having negative peer pressure (39 percent

and 27 percent, respectively) than whites (20 percent). The third most influential factor attributed to these arson delinquencies was family conflicts: 13 percent of both whites and blacks, compared to 8 percent of Hispanics, had family conflicts as their major adjustment problem.

5. The youngest arsonists (those aged eleven to sixteen) were more likely to live with just their natural mother or with a substitute mother (such as a stepmother, foster parents, or a guardian) than were the older firesetters (those seventeen years and older), who were more likely to live with both natural parents. Younger juveniles, it appears, are more likely to be negatively affected by broken homes than older juveniles and young adults.

6. Another statistically significant pattern showed that those arsonists diagnosed as having mental and emotional problems came from a wider variety of family arrangements (i.e., both natural parents, a single parent, a natural parent and a stepparent, a guardian or a foster home) than did those juveniles diagnosed as having either family conflicts or peer influences.

7. The youngest arsonists had the greatest number of family conflicts, and the arsonists who were in their mid-teens at the time of their offense had greater negative peer pressure. Those diagnosed with mental and emotional problems were less age-specific; in other words, these more troubled youngsters ranged in age from eleven to twenty-four.

8. Caucasian youths were more evenly distributed among all age categories. Blacks, on the other hand, were disproportionately either younger or older (compared to the middle age group) at the time of their arson incident. Hispanics were more

likely to be in the youngest age group (ages eleven to fifteen).

9. Among the youngest arsonists, those with mental and emotional adjustment problems were more likely to live with a natural parent and a stepparent. Those with negative peer influences were more likely to live with both natural parents.

In summary, based on our analysis of these 192 juvenile arsonists who were incarcerated in the California penal facilities, whites were more likely to be diagnosed as neurotic; to come from neighborhoods with little delinquency; to come from higher socioeconomic neighborhoods; to have more mental and emotional problems; and to be more varied in age. By contrast, both blacks and Hispanics (notably fewer in number than whites, as they collectively comprised only two-fifths of the total group) were more likely to be diagnosed as conformists; to come from more delinquent and lower socioeconomic neighborhoods; to have more negative peer pressure; and to be at the extreme ends of the age range (either younger or much older).

Besides these ethnic and racial differences, the age of the youngster at the time of incarceration was another significant variable distinguishing these firesetters. The younger arsonists in correctional institutions were more likely to have grown up in more varied family arrangements; to have a greater number of family conflicts; and to be diagnosed as having mental and emotional adjustment problems. The older CYA arsonists, on the other hand, had greater negative peer influence but lived with both natural parents.

In Chapter 12, we discuss, in some detail, the variety of treatment programs that the CYA employs with these arson offenders. There we present interviews that we conducted both with the psychologist who helped to develop the classification manual and with the psychiatrist and deputy director of one of the correctional facility treatment programs.

Here we present an interview that we conducted with a Catholic chaplain (who wished to remain unidentified) who worked for several years with the CYA wards, as well as a summary of discussions we had with other prison staff officials. The priest's comments reflect the frustration that many officials who work with these troubled juveniles expressed to us:

Q: Tell us about the juveniles you worked with. Were they receptive to religious counseling?

A: The ones I saw were aged from fourteen to twenty-five. Some would ask to see you. Some would use you. They would want you to send letters out to their family or to their girlfriends. One letter I tore up because it was so crazy.

Q: Did they want to clear their consciences?

A: Some are very clear of what they've done and want to rectify their mistakes. Others, no. They are so hardened, they don't know right from wrong.

Q: Were you of help to these kids?

A: You are completely frustrated—the helplessness of the situation. The staff was of no help. To them, the kids were animals. They made comments such as, "We got another load of garbage." But the staff didn't give us any problems. No wards cussed me or abused me. Even among the non-Catholic wards, they wanted to see the priest. I was reluctant because the Protestant priest [sic] was touchy.

Q: Have you kept in touch with any of the wards once they were released?

A: One, who seemed to be doing well. He got a job in a gas station.

Q: What was your impression of the kids?

A: Some were great; others were worthless. Some refused any kind of help. The place where I worked was in the reception center. You would never see the kids more than once or twice at the most. You would see them in the beginning of their incarceration and some would be very scared.

Q: Why do kids set fires?

A: In my opinion, to get attention. Either they want to be somebody or they need help.

Q: Any differences in the attitude of the girls?

A: They were about the same. A lot of kids realized they weren't going to be in the reception center that long.

Q: Any racial differences?

A: Very few blacks set fires. Mexicans were more dangerous than blacks. Mexicans would just as soon stab you as give you a cup of coffee.

Q: Should society treat youth separately from adults?

A: In some cases, they are so hardened there is no possibility of rehabilitation. The only way we have now is to stick them in a cell. With the first or second offense, we should try to do something with them, but with a third or fourth crime, and a serious crime like murder, you have to call it quits.

Q: What is the church's position on criminals and rehabilitation?

A: The church leans towards leniency and giving them every consideration.

Q: Were you asked to give input on the release of the wards?

A: Yes, very often I would sit in on the parole board and would be asked how I felt about a subject. I would provide a religious point of view, noting whether or not I felt the youngster had a moral conscience and what he felt about what he had done.

Q: How did you work with the juveniles?

A: My way was to let the kids talk and draw them out. They talked with me as long as they needed to before they'd return to their cell.

Q: Did you enjoy this assignment?

A: In the beginning, I did. But with time, I was frustrated. I was making no progress. Sometimes I'd see the same kids come back to the reception center [after they had been released]. After 3½ years I wanted to get out before I became completely bitter.

Q: Why do these kids go wrong?

A: Lousy home life. There was no father or their mother was a prostitute. Some had been "used" constantly and had no respect and fear of adults. They were used sexually, physically, and had even been forced to steal.

Q: Did you ever meet with their parents?

A: Once in a while. I'd go to the visiting room. For the most part, the parents were receptive.

Q: Did the wards see you as being on their side or on the side of the staff?

A: Both. Some would see you on one side or the other. I tried to stay away from sides and see what could make the kids' life better.

Q: How did you get assigned to the reception center?

A: Priests are assigned by bishops. The CYA notifies the chancellery office of a vacancy, and the office assigns us. Prison ministry is viewed as a prestigious assignment. One of the advantages is the salary, since in a parish, the salary is low. Today, for example, I get three hundred dollars a month plus room and board and the use of a car. With prison work you earn a higher salary as you are paid by the state.

Q: What's prison life like for these kids?

A: For Youth Authority wards, it's not all that bad.

Q: What is the church's view toward fire?

A: Allusions to fire are found in many biblical passages. Fire is viewed as redemption and purifier. Purgatory is pictured with "fire and brimstone," although now hell is more commonly viewed as the absence of the love of God. In church services, fire is used in the ceremony with the lighting of incense and candles.

Q: Have churches been deliberately set on fire?

A: One of the worst arson fires in Chicago had been a church fire where a good number of nuns were burned. With a church fire, the altar or altar linens are often ignited. In this area, one girl lit a fire and climbed naked on top of the altar. She was performing something like a "black mass" or satanic rite or parody of the Catholic Mass.

Q: Why do they set fire to the altar?

A: Because it is the central place of worship. If they are angry at the church, they set what is representative of the church.

Q: Over the years, have you noticed any changes in kids?

A: Kids change because life stresses change.

Q: What about the so-called latchkey children?

A: I can't imagine anything more destructive than a kid coming home to an empty house. There is no family interaction, no one to talk to. It is difficult for a family to give any interaction as they are never with their children long enough.

Q: Do children from lower socioeconomic backgrounds have different types of problems?

A: Some of the youngsters from Mexico have difficulty trying to accommodate to the culture of the United States. This is a problem with Mexican girls particularly. The parents can't fit into the life of these kids.

   The church now tries to take people as they are and not emphasize their assimilation and becoming American. But as a teacher, I was against bilingual eduation, and I still feel that way. It's better for kids to learn as much English in the natural way. When you give them bilingual education, they don't speak English when they get to high school, and they never make it to college. These school failures lead to their delinquency and firesetting.

   Interviews were also conducted with several staff members of three Youth Authority facilities. According to CYA authorities, there are currently 115 beds set aside for those juveniles—including arsonists—who are receiving specialized, intensive, therapeutic treatment. These beds are located in six separate correctional facilities.

Concurring with our findings, the staff members noted that, with respect to the severely disturbed firesetters, they were working with teenagers who were basically passive-aggressive and unassertive. Most of them had severe family problems, and their firesetting was viewed as the juveniles' means of expressing anger toward their parents.

One correctional institution director distinguished the arsonists from the other delinquents as being "pretty inadequate kids." He noted that physically the juvenile arsonists were not as strong as the others and that many of them looked "bizarre." Most were small in size, disjointed, weak, and, in the director's words, "almost grotesque." One correctional institution psychologist said, "Their bodies don't go together. If you split the top and bottom, or right and left sides, they would be 'out of whack.'" These observations, rather than reflecting the juveniles' actual physical features, may, instead, be indicative of the authorities' attitudes toward these kids.

Constitutional and physical factors, however, have been noted in past research on firesetters. A number of studies show a high incidence of chromosomal abnormalities in persons who set fires.[10] People with such abnormalities have been described as having poor coordination, a condition that might also make their social adjustment more difficult because they may face peer ridicule and rejection. None of the firesetters in our San Bernardino group, however, were diagnosed as having this problem.

The juvenile firesetters are also distinguished from the other CYA wards in their inability to play. They are not quite as free at horseplaying as other adolescents their age.

Further, they are viewed by the correctional officers as being anxious, immature, and passive.

According to the guards, many of these young males have "sexual identity" problems. Although not specifically homosexual in their sexual orientation, many of these male juvenile arsonists have had limited social—let alone sexual—experiences with members of the opposite sex. And as in the case of the younger "punks" in a correctional facility study that one of us conducted with Jay Parker,[11] these submissive youngsters are often sexually harassed in county jail, juvenile hall, and the various prison facilities by other, more sexually aggressive, males. These forced sexual situations merely exacerbate their own confusion about their sexual identity.

According to correctional facility officials, those juvenile arsonists who have been incarcerated for burning buildings for profit are more similar to delinquents who have been incarcerated for burglary and theft. Although no juvenile in our San Bernardino sample had been apprehended for being a "hired torch," there were several firesetters in the correctional institution population who had been apprehended for setting fires for monetary gain. Often, these youngsters had been hired by adults to set fire to establishments so that the owners could collect insurance. More commonly, however, the hired torch is an adult offender.

One CYA psychologist noted that many of the severely disturbed firesetters experience the world in "visual" ways and that this trait differentiates them from the other delinquents. For example, when these arsonists close their eyes, they frequently see fires, the color red, and the like. This staff member contends that their firesetting behavior is quite possibly related to these visual dependencies in that their emotional states are soothed and satisfied by fire-related imagery.

The San Bernardino County probation department is currently conducting research on the body chemistry and the hair analysis of these youngsters to see if their physiological state differs from that of youngsters who are delinquent in other ways, and from that of juveniles who are not delinquent. No conclusive findings have yet been reported.

In summary, according to the several staff members we interviewed, juvenile arsonists set fires as a means of compensating for their feelings of powerlessness. As one deputy director put it, "They watch fire as if they were watching pornography. They have an intense fascination and satisfaction with fire. And when they feel low or inadequate, they need merely to 'flick their Bic.'"

Chapter Ten

FROM FIREBUGS TO FIRE FIGHTERS?

Marin County sheriff's detectives arrested a volunteer fire fighter at the scene of a grass fire he is suspected of starting. Marinwood Fire Department volunteer, Randy Williams, 31, was taken into custody when he responded in fire fighting gear to help fight the blaze at an area three blocks from his home. Williams, suspected of arson in several other instances, had been under investigation by Marin County arson investigators and sheriff's detectives for 14 months.[1]

As a rookie fireman I had been on the job for less than three months when it was announced that the fire chiefs from several surrounding fire units were planning a mutual aid, tri-city, "hot drill." There were two large buildings that were slated for demolition. It was planned that we would stock the buildings with old furniture, lumber, mattresses, and tumbleweeds for a larger burn early one Saturday morning. Late in the day on Friday, we were told that our company would not be allowed to participate. My captain made the comment that we should burn the place down ourselves if they were not going to allow us to enjoy the fruits of our labor. I turned to him and said, "I'll torch it off for you."

When he saw that I was serious, he laid out a plan. We would wait until 2:00 A.M. because our chief was pulling guard duty till midnight. Then the assistant chief would relieve him until dawn. I would use a mixture of kerosene and diesel oil to prevent a premature explosive atmosphere. At 2:00 A.M. sharp, I drove down in my civilian car.

135

I saw that no one was around, turned off my lights, and pulled over just past the larger of the two buildings. With the engine running, I took my two five-gallon jerry cans and laid out a particular trail pattern. I put the empty cans back into the car and knelt down outside the doorway. (Arsonists have been badly burned, or killed, standing up while torching a fire that has been primed with a flamable liquid.) I lit my two flares and threw them in—one to the left, and one to the right. I got into my car and started back to the fire station two miles away.

Halfway back, I saw flames leaping out of the upstairs windows and got so excited and yelled aloud, that I darn near drove off the road. Just as I pulled into the fire station parking lot, the alarm bells rang. While the captain took the information, I kicked off my tennis shoes, pulled on my boots, put on my turnout coat and helmet, jumped on the back of the pumper, and drove with red lights and siren to *my* fire. Engine Company No. 2 got stuck in the soft dirt, and when the disappointed fire chief showed up, he told us, "Just let the damn thing burn." Our fire inspectors found some clear footprints indicating the sole of a tennis shoe. A Los Angeles arson investigator was called in on Saturday afternoon and made plaster-of-paris casts of the prints, and he also found one of the spent flares. The fire chief was understandably upset and vowed that he would get the responsible individual(s) and have their job. I was a little bit worried.

A year later, I got over my fear because my probation was up. I planned to mail my tennis shoes, anonymously, to the fire chief from one of the desert cities, just to bear a phony postmark. When my captain heard about this, he took the shoes and burned them, telling me that we could all lose our jobs if the truth were known.

In 1980, two years after the fire chief retired, he was told what really happened. At a meeting, the old chief stood up and said that he could not believe that his own buddies would do something like that to him. He left the room, and a few minutes later, he returned with the plaster cast. They told him that it was my footprint, and he just shook his head. The best kept secret for twenty years had come out, and to this day he still will not discuss it with me. (Comments from a fire captain)

One striking pattern among the young firesetters we studied was their interest in becoming fire fighters when they became adults. Many of the boys, aged seven and under, frequently indicated that they liked to pretend that they were fire fighters and mentioned that their favorite play toy was a fire truck. The older adolescent males, when asked, often said that they would like the excitement of being a fire fighter.

According to fire department officials, some boys set fires to attract their fire fighter role models. Lacking attention at home, these preteenage males are drawn to fire and fire fighters as some other juveniles are drawn to athletics and their coaches or Boy Scouts and their scoutmasters. Fire play, for these troubled youngsters, is a deviant form of male adolescents' play and identification with male role models.

Noting this pattern in several of our firesetters, we decided to study one fire department in the San Bernardino area to see if the fire fighters themselves thought that fire fighters, in general, had had a history of firesetting behavior as juveniles. In other words, we wanted to know if firesetters grow up to become fire fighters. We also questioned these fire fighters about such things as why they thought juveniles in general set fires, and whether or not their own children (or siblings) had set fires.

The first comprehensive study to look at the arsonist behavior of fire "buffs," "would-be" fire fighters, and "volunteer" fire fighters was the 1951 project conducted by psychologists Lewis and Yarnell.[2] In that study, the fire "buffs" were identified as the enthusiastic "hangers-on" who like to be around fires, fire fighters, and fire houses. Although seemingly civic-minded and constructive, these type of fire "buffs" set fires. According to the authors, they are characteristically immature and inadequate and are underachievers. They seek attention and attempt in a pathological way to win praise for their assistance in fighting the fires they have set.

Often, these "buffs" are similar to the "would-be" fire fighters who attract attention to themselves by setting fires so that they can play the would-be hero. These "vanity" firesetters are described by Drs. Lewis and Yarnell as "men with grandiose social ambitions whose natural equipment [meaning physiological and psychological constitution] dooms them to insignificance." Included in this category are the men who set fires so that they can demonstrate how clever they are. Setting fires offers an opportunity to achieve community recognition for turning in an alarm or helping the fire fighters. The researchers found that 6 percent of their sample group were would-be hero firesetters.

Another 4 percent of their arsonists were "volunteer" fire fighters, who work only under emergency conditions and are not hired as full-time employees. The volunteer may be either a paid or an unpaid worker. These types may wish to impress their families or their superiors with their performance and set fires to give themselves more opportunity to do so. Sometimes, their motive is purely monetary, as they know they will be paid to fight the fire.

One textbook on arson investigation argues that with this type of firesetter, the investigation should focus on a background check of current personnel, especially those who either reported or helped extinguish the fire. Furthermore, recently rejected applicants for the position of fire fighter should be considered potential suspects, as their attention-seeking fire may be set out of their frustrated ambitions to become a fire fighter.[3]

The fire department we selected to study celebrated its diamond anniversary in 1980. Although part-time volunteer fire fighters have performed services in the community for some seventy-five years, the department has been in full-time operation only since 1955. This pattern has been typical for most of the San Bernardino County fire departments, as population increases in this region of the country have been a post–World War II phenomenon.

In its infancy, the department's activity was primarily fire suppression. Today, its programs have expanded to include not only fire prevention, emergency operations training, and paramedic services and rescue operations, but also family and juvenile counseling when firesetting incidents have occurred. Working closely with the San Bernardino County Probation Department, this fire department has developed a three-person fire-education and counseling program that administers, among other things, the classification manual to the families of juvenile firesetters. For this reason, we have turned to this atypical, progressive fire department for our study.

Improved fire safety and prevention, according to the department's own 1980 annual report, account for a decrease in the deaths of citizens from fire, despite a continued increase in population. This decline to two to four deaths per year is attributed to more people installing smoke detectors in their home. With no fire-fighter fatalities for several years, and with a decrease in injuries to both fire fighters and citizens, the fire department boasts of its success in early fire detection and prevention.

Even with such successes, however, the fire fighters have their work cut out for them. In the year 1980, for example, there were nearly 7,000 emergency responses. Most of these emergencies were in the area of paramedic calls. The department now employs a fire-fighting force of 151 men and 1 woman, as well as a support staff of 18 who are located in the main station and three satellite stations.

One important development, critical to our study of juvenile arsonists, is the department's stepping up of fire investigations and juvenile counseling. Although the fire department had been involved in counseling and fire prevention in the past, not until 1980 did it begin to assign fire personnel—who had taken special training workshops and college courses in clinical and counseling psychology—to work specifically with the families of youngsters who had been apprehended by the fire department for setting fires. Because the fire personnel are not trained clinical psychologists or psychiatrists, they work only with the less disturbed youngsters. In the case of the more serious offender, they make arrangements for the family to meet with an appropriate certified therapist.

The number of juvenile firesetters counseled in this program increased from 128 in 1979 to 210 youngsters in 1980, its first year of expansion. The department currently assigns a high priority to this fire-safety and counseling program, as they see its benefit in decreasing adolescent firesetting.

Furthermore, a comparison with the mid-1950s, when the department was in its infancy, demonstrates the marked increase in all fire-related services. For example, the number of "alarm fires" (fires called into the fire station) in 1955 was 510. This figure had more than doubled by 1980, when there were 1,042 alarm fires reported. Further, in 1955, only 16 children were counseled for "playing with matches," compared to the 210 children so counseled in 1980. The lower figure in 1955 may reflect a lower priority given to the fire safety program at that time. It also may indicate that firesetting behavior by juveniles either occurred less frequently or was less often brought to the attention of the authorities. Nevertheless, with slightly more than a doubling of the city's population in the past twenty-five years to 88,820 in 1980, an alarming 1,213 percent increase in that same time period in the number of juvenile arsonists indicates that the city has a new and major problem on its hands.

To gain a better understanding of the attitudes and behavior of municipal fire fighters, we decided to conduct a study in 1983 on this "Blazer" Fire Department. With the assistance of the fire captain in charge of the department's fire safety program, we administered a lengthy questionnaire to all 170 personnel in the department. This study, furthermore, had the complete support of the fire chief. The questionnaire was printed under the city seal of the Blazer Fire Department with a request by the fire captain that all fire fighters participate in the study. They completed, and anonymously returned, a total of 128 questionnaires, which represented a response rate of 75 percent. (A copy of the questionnaire is included in Appendix A.)

Several background questions were asked of the fire fighters, including their sex; ethnic or racial identification; age; years of service; level of education; current marital status; current rank in the department; religious affiliation, if any; and their father's occupation.

In terms of *sex*, all but 1 of the 128 firefighters who completed the questionnaire were male. In terms of *ethnic or racial identification*, Caucasians represented 90 percent of the sample. The Blazer Fire Department had 114 whites, 3 blacks, and 9 Hispanics. Two fire fighters did not report their ethnicity.

By *age* groupings, one-third (33 percent) of the respondents indicated that they were under thirty years of age, and only two fire fighters indicated that they were under twenty-three. Two-fifths (41 percent) were between thirty and forty, and one-fourth (26 percent) were over forty. Only five in the department were over fifty years of age.

With respect to *years of service*, slightly more than one-third (37 percent) had been fire fighters for less than six years. Nearly one-third (31 percent) had served between six and ten years, and two-fifths (41 percent) had worked as fire fighters for over ten years (including 11 percent who had been fire fighters for over twenty years).

As to *level of education*, all but two of the respondents had been educated beyond a high-school degree. Close to half (47 percent) had the equivalent of a two-year junior college education, and close to half (48 percent) had achieved schooling beyond two years in college. Four had graduated from a four-year college program, and three had attended graduate school.

In terms of *current marital status*, nearly three-quarters (74 percent) indicated that they were married, with the remainder indicating that they were either single (14 percent) or divorced (12 percent).

In response to *current rank* in the department, over one-third (38 percent) listed that they were of the rank of fire fighter (lowest rank). In ascending order by rank (based on type of duties performed, degree of responsibility, level of education, and amount of time served in the department), the remainder listed paramedic (7 percent), captain (43 percent), battalion or division chief (9 percent), or fire chief (3 percent) as their current rank in the department.

As to *religious affiliation*, over half (54 percent) listed Protestant as their faith. The remainder listed either Catholic (17 percent) or other faith (17 percent) or responded that they were atheist (12 percent).

Finally, in terms of their own *father's occupation*, most of those who responded to this question listed occupations that would categorize their fathers as blue-collar workers or working-class (45 percent). One-fifth (21 percent) of the respondents listed white-collar or middle-class occupations for their fathers, and a few (5 percent) listed their father's occupation as being of the professional or upper middle class. Over one-quarter (29 percent) of the respondents, however, did not report their father's occupation.

In summary, the "typical" profile of the Blazer Fire Department fire fighter was as follows: a male Caucasian in his thirties; with six to ten years of service as a fire fighter; with some college education; married; of the rank of either fire fighter or captain; of the Protestant faith; and generally from a blue-collar or working-class background.

Our study asked twenty-five questions concerning the fire fighters' attitudes toward juveniles who set fires, their job as fire fighters, arson in general, and, more specifically, the firesetting behavior of fire fighters and their own children. To each of these questions, the respondents were given the choice of response: "strongly agree," "agree," "not sure," "disagree," or "strongly disagree." For our purposes here, the two "agree" categories were combined, as were the two "disagree" categories. (Table B-20 provides a summary table of the fire fighters' responses to these twenty-five statements.)

We included four statements in the questionnaire to explore the reasons that they thought children set fires.

One such statement was "Juveniles who set fires do so as a means of 'crying for help.'" Close to half (47 percent) of the respondents agreed with this statement, one-fourth (24 percent) indicated they were not sure, and one-fourth (29 percent) disagreed.

A second statement was "Kids who set fires are just basically curious." This statement elicited similar responses to the preceding statement. Close to half (46 percent) agreed with the statement, and the remainder either indicated that they were not sure (21 percent) or disagreed with the statement (33 percent).

Another statement read, "Kids who set fires are delinquents." There were more respondents, interestingly, who disagreed (48 percent) with this statement than either agreed (21 percent) or were not sure (31 percent). In other words, the fire fighters felt that juveniles who set fires do so because they are basically curious (46 percent) and/or they are "crying for help" (47 percent), but *not* because they are delinquents (21 percent).

Likewise, in response to the statement "Adolescents who get into trouble are more likely to be firesetters," only a third (29 percent) of the respondents were in agreement, a third (32 percent) indicated that they were not sure, and the remaining third (39 percent) disagreed. Although the respondents were more evenly divided on this statement, it appears that, to these fire fighters, children who set fires are not necessarily delinquents, nor do troubled adolescents necessarily become firesetters. Firesetting behavior in children, to reiterate, appears to be related to, according to these fire fighters, a child's basic curiosity or a "cry for help." In this regard, the fire fighters appeared to hold a more humanistic approach to why children engage in firesetting behavior than might be expected.

Another series of questions asked the fire fighters to comment on their job. According to our interview with the fire captain of this department, spouses of fire fighters who are newly hired are brought together so that discussions can take place about the demands that a fire fighter's job makes on his or her family, and those stresses to which the spouses are particularly susceptible. According to this fire captain, fire fighters, in general, have heavy drinking problems, engage in gambling, have frequent family problems, and engage in extramarital affairs—all of which create work, staff, and family problems.

Nine questions were asked of the respondents concerning their job as fire-safety personnel.

One statement asked if they agreed or disagreed that "Fire fighters are underpaid." The vast majority (86 percent) felt that they were underpaid. Only a small percentage either stated they were not sure (5 percent) or disagreed (9 percent) with the statement.

Another statement said, "Fire fighters are overworked in their job." Only a comparatively small percentage (18 percent) agreed with this statement, and the same percentage (18 percent) indicated they were not sure. By contrast, close to two-thirds (64 percent) disagreed, indicating that they did not feel that fire fighters were overworked. Some, however, did feel that they were both overworked *and* underpaid.

According to various fire department administrators, these findings reflect a common point of view (which our data support) that fire fighters consider themselves grossly underpaid for the high risks they take on their job, but not necessarily overworked.

Another point raised was "Fire fighters experience less stress than police officers." Only a comparatively small percentage (20 percent) agreed with this statement or indicated that they were not sure (15 percent). Close to two-thirds (65 percent) disagreed with the statement, indicating that they experienced as much stress as (or possibly more than) police officers. According to the fire captain, the fire fighters are particularly sensitive to this topic because many of them perceive that the general public does not think that fire fighters have as consistently difficult a job to perform as police officers.

Another statement concerning stress was "Fire fighters deal with stress in nonproductive ways." Interestingly, close to half of the respondents (45 percent) agreed, indicating that they did *not* deal with stress well. The remaining half either indicated that they were not sure (21 percent) or disagreed (34 percent) with the statement.

Because job-related stress is a major factor in the lives of fire fighters, in late 1983 the Los Angeles City Fire Department introduced a series of biofeedback and holistic techniques to their recruits. The results of this "Alpha-Learning Program" are not yet available; however, other fire departments, including the Blazer Department, are receptive to the program because stress in fire fighters is a primary administrative concern.

Another statement in our study was "Fire fighters, in general, enjoy going to fires." As expected, a majority (85 percent) reported that they did enjoy going to fires. Only a small percentage indicated that they were not sure (9 percent) if they enjoyed going to fires or disagreed (6 percent) with the statement. In this sense, as fire fighters, these people appear to enjoy their work, as their work obviously involves going to fires. Also, the rest of their time is often spent doing nothing; thus, going to fires must relieve their boredom.

The fire captain agreed with this finding, and stated, "You should see this place when the alarm sounds, the faces on the men. Finally, at last, they have a fire. This is particularly true when we've had a fire drought."

Not all the fire fighters, however, indicated that they enjoyed going to fires. In a comparison of responses by those who reported handling stress in nonproductive ways and enjoying going to fires, the results, although not statistically significant, were that those who did not enjoy going to fires *also* indicated that they did not deal with stress productively. Part of the reason for their stress might therefore be a dislike of their job.

Several questions were asked of the fire fighters concerning relationships with their family members. One statement, for instance, was "Spouses of fire fighters generally do not understand the demands of their spouse's job." Close to half of the respondents (46 percent) felt, in fact, that their spouses did *not* understand the demands of their jobs and so agreed with the statement. A like percentage (44 percent) disagreed with the statement; only a small number (10 percent) were not sure. Thus, those who were married appeared to be evenly split over whether or not their spouses understood the demands of their job.

In a related statement, the respondents read, "Family members of fire fighters are supportive of the fire fighter's profession." There was near unanimous agreement with this statement. Nearly all of the fire fighters (93 percent) felt that they had the support of their family members. Only a small percentage (5 percent) were not sure or disagreed (2 percent) with the statement.

When comparing the responses to these last two statements, unique patterns emerged. A sizable number of respondents (45 percent) agreed both that their family was supportive and that their spouses did not understand the demands of their job. We questioned the fire captain about this seeming contradiction, and he replied that most spouses do not understand the work because most fire fighters either play down the hazards, or simply do not communicate the details of the job. Fire fighters, he claimed, are three times more likely than the general public to develop heart and lung disease because of the stress of the job and the chemicals and other materials they occasionally ingest while fighting fires. Their kids, according to this official, are supportive because most youngsters see only the excitement of racing to a fire, climbing on the roof, or going inside the burning building and rescuing people.

Two other items concerning the job were on the questionnaire. One statement was "Fire fighters are generally extraverted people." Close to three-fifths (59 percent) of the respondents agreed with the statement; the remainder indicated that they were not sure (20 percent) or disagreed (21 percent). The majority of the fire fighters felt that they were outgoing and enjoyed being with people.

The last item stated, "Fire fighters understand kids who set fires more than the average citizen would." The fire fighters were divided on this issue. Although the plurality agreed (45 percent) that fire fighters do understand the firesetting behavior of kids better than the average citizen, many respondents either indicated that they were not sure (26 percent) or disagreed (29 percent) with the statement. Being a fire fighter, it appears, does *not* naturally make an individual more competent in understanding why juveniles engage in firesetting.

To summarize these findings concerning their job, fire fighters felt that they were underpaid but not necessarily overworked. They felt that they experienced as much stress as police officers. Many of them felt that they did not deal with stress productively. Most fire fighters enjoyed going to fires. They felt that although their family members were supportive of their careers, their spouses did not fully understand the demands of their job. The respondents considered fire fighters basically extraverted. And they did not necessarily understand, any better than the average citizen, why children set fires.

Several questions were asked concerning the levels of arson in this country. One statement was "Arson in America is on the decrease." Only a small number (9 percent) agreed with this statement. The vast majority (81 percent) did not believe that arson was on the decrease. A small group (10 percent) indicated that they were not sure.

Another statement was "Juvenile arson in this country is on the increase." Agreement with this statement was less uniform. Only a little more than three-fifths (62 percent) agreed, whereas close to one-third (30 percent) indicated that they were not sure or disagreed (8 percent).

It is interesting to note that although the fire fighters felt that arson in America was not decreasing, they were not as strong in their opinion that juvenile arson was increasing. In fact, some of the respondents (11 percent) actually felt that juvenile arson was decreasing although arson in America was increasing overall.

One statement was "Intervention programs for juvenile firesetters are properly a function of the fire department." Exactly three-fifths (60 percent) of the respondents felt that such programs were a function of fire departments, although one-fifth (21 percent) indicated that they were not sure, and one-fifth (19 percent) disagreed with the statement. Those who appeared to be most in agreement with the need for such intervention programs also were the most likely to agree with the earlier statement that kids who set fires are doing so as a means of "crying for help."

Four key items dealt with more personal matters, such as the firesetting behavior of fire fighters when they were juveniles, as well as the firesetting behavior of their own offspring, and that of fire fighters' offspring in general.

One statement focused on the following, "Fire fighters, as compared to non-fire-fighters, have very likely had a history of firesetting." Three-quarters (72 percent) of the respondents disagreed with this statement. Some, however, either indicated that they were not sure (19 percent) or agreed (9 percent). That is, some fire fighters ($N = 11$) felt that fire fighters in general *have* had a history of arson activity themselves. We should bear in mind, however, that the fire fighters who shared this belief were in the minority.

In looking more closely at this group that indicated that fire fighters in general have very likely had a history of firesetting behavior, several statistically significant findings emerged. For instance, these men had these other

beliefs in common (listed in decreasing levels of significance):

1. They believed that fire fighters are extraverted.
2. They agreed with the statement that their own
   firesetting behavior in childhood was no different
   from that of average youngsters.
3. They disagreed with the statement that children of
   fire personnel are *less* likely to set trouble fires.

Furthermore, those who agreed that fire fighters in
general have very likely had a history of firesetting behavior also shared these general (though not significant)
patterns:

1. They had a higher level of education.
2. They believed that adolescents who get into trouble
   are *more* likely to be firesetters.
3. They believed that fire fighters, more than the average citizen, can understand kids who set fires.

A specific statement concerning their own firesetting
behavior was given these Blazer fire fighters: "My own
firesetting behavior as a youngster was no different from
the average kid's." Over half (55 percent) agreed with the
statement, and some (18 percent) indicated that they were
not sure. Only a small number (9 percent) disagreed, although another group (18 percent) felt that the statement
was not applicable to them.

In looking specifically at the responses of those fire
fighters (55 percent) who indicated that as children their
own firesetting behavior was no different from that of the
average youngster, several significant patterns emerged.
The fire fighters who agreed with this statement shared
these other beliefs (in decreasing levels of significance):

1. They believed that fire fighters in general have had
   a history of firesetting behavior.

2. They believed that kids who set fires do so as a means of "crying for help."
3. They disagreed with the statement that children of fire personnel are *less* likely to set trouble fires.
4. They believed that juvenile arson activity in this country is on the increase.

Two questions specifically addressed the issue of the firesetting behavior of the children of fire fighters. One statement read, "Children of fire personnel are less likely to set trouble fires." Half the respondents (51 percent) agreed that children of fire personnel are *less* likely to set such fires. The other half, however, either indicated that they were not sure (27 percent) or disagreed with the statement (23 percent). Thus, nearly one-quarter of the fire fighters believed either that children of fire personnel were as likely to set fires as children of non-fire-fighters or were, in fact, more likely to set fires.

One last question asked specifically about the firesetting behavior of their own offspring. The statement read, "My own kids (or younger siblings) have played with fire against my wishes." A comparatively small but nevertheless significant number of the fire fighters agreed that their kids had played with fire against their wishes (15 percent). Some (14 percent) indicated that they were not sure, and one-third of the respondents (35 percent) disagreed with the statement, and another one-third (36 percent) responded that the statement was not applicable to their situation.

Some interesting patterns emerged when the responses of those who agreed that their own kids had played with fire against their wishes were compared with their responses on other questions. Those fire fighters (15 percent) who agreed that their own children had set fires also had other common characteristics (in decreasing levels of significance):

1. They disagreed with the statement that children of fire personnel are *less* likely to set trouble fires.
2. They agreed with the statement that as children, their own firesetting behavior was no different from that of the average kid.
3. They were likely to be divorced.

Some of these patterns need further elaboration. In terms of the fire fighters' current marital status and whether their own children had set fires, two times more divorced fire fighters (31 percent) than married fire fighters (16 percent) indicated that their children *had* played with fire against their wishes.

Furthermore, as Table B-21 documents, a surprising 10 percent (13 of 123) of the Blazer fire fighters who indicated that their own firesetting behavior in childhood was no different from that of the average child had children who had played with fire against their wishes.

In summary, according to the fire fighters surveyed, a small group (9 percent) felt that fire fighters, as compared to non-fire-fighters, have very likely had a history of firesetting; an additional group (19 percent) were undecided about this. A majority of the fire fighters (55 percent) felt that their own firesetting behavior in childhood was no different from that of the average kid. With respect to the question on the firesetting behavior of the children of fire personnel, nearly one-fourth (23 percent) felt that such children were *not* less likely to set fires. And in terms of their own children's firesetting behavior, some respondents (15 percent) indicated that their children had played with fire against their wishes.

In looking more closely at the interrelationships of all these issues, an interesting pattern emerges. It appears that fire fighters who have, in the past, set trouble fires themselves are likely to believe that other fire fighters have had a history of setting fires. Furthermore, these people, if married, appear more likely to have troubled marriages (leading to separation and divorce) and to have children who have set fires against their wishes. They are also likely to believe that the children of fire personnel, in general, are not necessarily less likely to set fires than children of non-fire-fighters.

It is possible, therefore, to raise the following question: Could it not be argued that juvenile firesetting behavior, indicative of earlier interpersonal difficulties (as we discussed in previous chapters), may be related to later marital difficulties and general family problems, out of which come offspring who perpetuate the cycle of being troubled firesetters? In other words, some juveniles set fires because of a problem home life; they grow up and pursue careers as fire fighters; they marry but continue to have problems, which lead to divorce or separation; and their children, in the meantime, are subjected to a troubled home life and turn to setting fires. Thus, in a pattern common to family systems theory, a family disturbance—and the behavior it elicits (in this case, arson)—continues from one generation to the next.

Although the number of fire fighters to fit this general pattern and composite profile (10 percent) was small and was definitely a minority within the fire department studied, its presence was nevertheless startling.

We were unable to conduct an interview with a fire fighter who exactly fit this composite profile and was willing to talk with us about it. We were, however, able to interview one of the fire fighters of the department who fit some of the characteristics. He had set fires himself as a child (though not major fires); he was divorced; and his son had, over the years, set several fires.

This man was born in Southern California but had moved with his family to Texas when he was three years old. In Texas, his mother separated from his father for a short period of time. Once reconciled, the family returned to California. He is thirty-eight years old, has an older brother who is also a fire fighter, two older sisters, and a younger brother. He grew up in a working-class environment, and his father was employed in a series of odd jobs, such as driving a truck, farming for other people, and working as a mechanic in a garage:

Q: Did you set any fires that you remember when you were a kid?

A: I'm sure I did, but it doesn't stand out in my mind. Nothing that I got caught with. I never set a fire that I remember in a house or anything like that, but I'm sure as a child I must have set fires outside.

Q: Did you notice any of your brothers or sisters setting fires?

A: No, I didn't notice that.

Q: Did you grow up going camping and hiking and things like that? Or were you part of Boy Scouts, where firesetting behavior might have been taught to you in appropriate ways?

A: I did a lot of hunting and I knew how to set a fire.

Q: At what age do you remember possibly wanting to become a fire fighter?

A: I was twenty-two. My brother had already become a fire fighter, and he started bugging me about it. Before that, I had hoped to use my athletic and scholastic scholarships, but with my father's death, a lot of my plans went to the wayside. I had a feeling of some sort of responsibility for my mother and my younger brother, and so I stayed at home. After I got out of high school, I worked for an electric company.

Q: How long have you been in this fire department?

A: Thirteen years. I was twenty-five when I started.

Q: When did you get married?

A: I was nineteen. I met my first wife through church. At that time in my life, I was very much involved with church activities. I taught Sunday school and even gave a few sermons. I admired our preacher, and it was his daughter who became my first wife.

Q: Did you date each other over a period of time?

A: No, not really. I had been going with another girl. We were high-school sweethearts, but we had a falling out and were broken up at the time. This other young lady was infatuated by me and more or less followed me around. Human nature being what it is, we had relations and she told me she was pregnant. I found out later that she wasn't pregnant but had only used it as a ploy to get me to marry her. She actually didn't become pregnant until the time we were married. When I found this out, it made me angry, which didn't make our relationship any stronger.

Q: What was the relationship like?

A: We were married for five years. In the beginning, I was very upset because I felt like I got hooked. I didn't want to be married. I had married her with the understanding that, after the baby was born, I would leave her. That's what I was going to do, but after a while it wasn't so bad. She wanted to have more children right away, but though I was willing to accept the situation as it was, I was not ready to commit myself that much to another child.

Q: What was your son like?

A: Beautiful. He was a real good kid. I had no problems with him. He was as "good as gold" when I was around. I thought we were close.

Q: What led to your divorce when he was five?

A: I think a lot of it was my attitude. I was still a very young man. I probably emotionally abused my wife by not having the affection for her that she wanted. After she started working, I found out that she had had a few sexual relationships, and that upset me. We separated over this but got back together and tried it again. She still resented my lack of feelings toward her and filed for a divorce. I didn't

want the divorce by that time because I didn't want to lose
my son.

Q: How did your son respond to the divorce?

A: In the beginning, he was very hostile. I know he resented
our separating.

Q: It was at this time that your son began setting fires. Will
you discuss these fires?

A: The first time it occurred, he and his mother were living in
this city. I had been in the fire department for maybe a year
or so. I was seeing my son as often as possible, although
not enough, I admit. It was probably my fault as much as
anything because of the new career and my going through
the fire academy, studying, and so forth. I'm sure he missed
me. I know I missed him. The first time it occurred, it was
a fire in their home. In talking with my son, and in having
other fire fighters in the department talk with him, it was
felt that it was his way of trying to get me to come back
home. He was about six-and-a-half or seven.

   The next fire occurred a few years later. He was probably nine or ten. That fire was a different story all together.
I think that it was more of a combativeness. He was getting
back at both me and his mother for not being together. By
then my ex-wife had remarried, and though he didn't dislike his stepfather, he wanted his mother and me to get
back together.

Q: What kind of fire did he set?

A: It was in a bedroom, in a closet, and then he left. I mean,
he knew what he was doing. It wasn't an accident. This
second fire, I think, was like his anger was coming out.

Q: Was anyone else in the house?

A: I don't believe so. I don't believe anyone was home.

Q: And the next fire after that?

A: There was another fire, but I can't remember where it fell.
It was out in the yard type-of-thing, and he always claimed,
even until much later, that it wasn't him. That it was set
by other kids.

Q: That second fire, had his mother had a new child?

A: Yes, she had had another child between his two fires.

Q: Any other problem fires?

A: There was a firecracker incident at school. He was a sophomore in high school. A teacher saw him with the firecracker and apprehended him. He was out of school for a couple of days and had to be counseled.

He's a senior now and lives with his mother, his stepfather, and their two children in Utah. I haven't seen him in quite a while. Two years ago, when they moved to Utah, he didn't want to go because of being away from his friends. When they got to Utah, he ran away. He was gone for a little while. I had to go to Utah to find him. I have thought about that a lot since, and my [second] wife seems to think that part of that was to get me up there. When I found him, I brought him back down here.

Q: What was your son like when he came down here to stay with you and your second wife?

A: Pretty good. He didn't like some of my rules, and it took a few weeks of adjustment. After six or seven months, he went back. This was more from his mother's and stepfather's persuasion than, I think, his really wanting to go back.

Q: What kind of grades did he get in high school? Any plans for him when he graduates?

A: He's a very intelligent young man. He could get A's anytime he wanted. He doesn't seem like he's interested in going to college at this time.

Q: Has he ever been really angry at you?

A: You mean openly hostile? We've sat down and talked. I have a temper, but I sat down with him, and I've never banged him around. I won't say never; I did, too. You know, once when he was playing little league and he got out, I took him up against the wall, threatened him a little bit, but I've never really whaled on him.

Q: The firecracker incident occurred during the period he was staying with you, right?

A: Yes, he had lived all this time in Utah and then came back, and it was here that he set the firecracker.

Q: Did you see any reason that that behavior would occur here
     as opposed to Utah?

A: I didn't see it as anything but a high-school thing. In talking
     with him after he had been counseled by the fire depart-
     ment, I didn't see any relationship between his setting off
     fires when he was younger and the firecracker incident.

Q: What's he like in terms of what he likes to do? Is he quiet
     or moody? Is he tall, lanky? Was he awkward as a kid? You
     were athletic by comparison.

A: He's moody. When he was here during that seven-month
     period, it was very difficult to get him to actually sit down
     and be open and talk. You know kids at that age; they don't
     want to respond. He's going to be tall. He was probably
     five foot ten at the time of the firecracker incident, so it
     depends on what you call tall. He is probably going to wind
     up being about six foot four; he's about six foot two now.
     I don't see him as awkward. He was not the athlete I was,
     but I tried not to say, "I did it, why can't you?"

Q: More general questions now. From our study, it appears
     that roughly 10 percent of the fire fighters in your depart-
     ment said that their own kids had set trouble fires. Do you
     find that sort of thing surprising?

A: No, I would have thought it would be higher. Maybe be-
     cause of my own experience, but I would think that chil-
     dren, missing their father and knowing he is a fireman,
     might set fires as a ploy to get their father to come to their
     location or home. This is true when the parents are sepa-
     rated or divorced.

Q: What might be some other reasons? Could it be sort of an
     embarrassment to their father, or a resentment?

A: If there was anger to the father, maybe.

Q: But in your case, you didn't see it as anger?

A: I didn't see it that way. I thought of it as his wanting me
     back. It was his call to try to get me there.

Q: Have you talked to other fire fighters whose kids have set
     fires? Have any other fire fighters mentioned it to you?

A: Not really. It's something you don't discuss. I have never really questioned other guys about it at all. It seems a little embarrassing from a fire fighter's standpoint to admit that your own child has set fires because you would think you would be a little more fire-safety-conscious.

We had the opportunity to question the deputy fire chief of the Blazer Fire Department about the results of our questionnaire. The department's cooperation in agreeing to our conducting this study was due in large measure to the interest of the department's administration in its findings:

Q: From the study, we found that many of the fire fighters, specifically those whose kids had set fires, were separated or divorced.

A: You'll find that probably the majority of fire fighters, period, are separated. Statistics show that we have probably one of the highest, if not *the* highest, divorce ratings as far as an occupation. [This statement could not be confirmed.] We're away from home twenty-four hours a whack, which makes it hard on families, spouses, everything. It takes a special person to be able to understand and put up with that.

Q: Do you think that fire fighters, have set fires in the past?

A: I would say probably so. Probably a great many.

Q: Do you think that fire fighters might set fires while they are fire fighters, as opposed to setting fires while they were kids?

A: I think there are those around. I would like to believe not so much on paid fire departments, but on volunteer departments. We read about it all the time. This has been proven. When times are slack or slow they're going to set one so they can get a run, or even to make themselves look like a hero.

I don't think this is common to the full-time professional fire fighter. We see fire from a different aspect. The volunteer might have some knowledge about how to manipulate the fire hose and so forth, and gets the thrill of responding when the bell goes off, but maybe doesn't relate that to what possibly could happen from a false alarm or an arson fire. But we professionals see people getting trapped and hurt in fires, and I can't see someone that is involved that much even attempting to set fires. I think they would have such a guilty conscience if something did happen, it would kill them.

Q: Do you think that children of fire fighters become fire fighters themselves, or do they choose a career totally opposite from what their parents do?

A: We have both types. I think that most fire fighters try to discourage their kids from coming in for several reasons. For one, they want their kids to do better than they have done. Also, they don't want them to get involved in dangerous situations.

Q: Tell me what it is like being a fire fighter and going to fires. Why do fire fighters enjoy fires?

A: Because that is what you are trained for. Fire fighters have been trained from Day One, whenever they see fire that automatically the fire must be put out. So fire fighters get that feeling that just builds up inside of them. And there is the thrill of driving to the fire. Everybody pulls off to the side of the road and you go through. Everybody is running out of the building and you go in. Everybody is running away from the building, and you put ladders up there and climb up on a roof. You're the person that is standing out there and everybody is looking up in awe at you. No one else knows what to do and you have the solution. You're the one in charge telling everybody what to do and how to do it.

Q: Do you think that fire fighters taking kids who have set fires *to* fires as a learning experience might be a way to curb their firesetting behavior?

A: I doubt it. I think it is just going to stir up some more excitement, more curiosity. I think showing a child the results of a fire can get better results.

Q: Do you think that fire departments should be involved with counseling kids and preventing firesetting behavior?

A: We are attempting to. This is why we are getting in on this program of counseling. This is why we are working with you so we can develop some type of program that can put these kids on a better path. One of the problems I see is that most of us feel inadequate to counsel some young child. We're not psychiatrists or psychologists, and we don't know whether we are getting the proper response from the child. And we don't really realize a lot of times what to say to that child. And we don't know what to do with the information when we get it.

Q: Your own department's research indicates that the number of children "playing with matches" has increased between 1979 and 1980, so there is a need for these types of programs.

A: This is coming about because the word is getting out to parents that we will counsel their kids if they have a problem. Kids who we would have no way of knowing have set fires are being brought into the department for counseling. Years ago, the method of interrogating kids who had set fires was to get them off on the side and say, "Look, you little bastard, I know you set the fire." This one inspector would do this. He would get angry and grab the kid by the shoulder and say, "Don't tell me any lies because I'll take you down and I'll lock you up, understand? Let me see your hands?" And then he'd tell the kids something about they had a test that they could give these kids to see if there was any carbon material on their fingers. The kids would begin to cry, and later he would say to me, "If you don't scare the hell out of them, they'll go out and set more fires." And that was truly his belief, that it was his job to scare the hell out of these kids.

Q: What is your reaction when a fire, either set by children or involving children, ends in death or severe destruction?

A: Frustration and anger. My first reaction is "What were the parents doing? Why wasn't there more of a control, es-

pecially if it involves little kids." I feel that the parents ought
to know where kids are and keep an eye on them. I don't
think that you're going to be able to teach children from
Day One never to touch fire, never play with fire, but
you've got to teach them to respect a fire, and what it can
do and the harmful aspects of it.

We had a fire downtown where we lost two little kids
in a trailer. The mother was working in a restaurant and
she got off work at something like 4:00 A.M. These kids were
already dead at about 2:00 A.M. She had left the kids with
her brother, who had got drunk, who had started a fire in
the kitchen to boil some hotdogs. There was a young girl
with the brother. She went to get the kids, but he told her
to get out of the way, that he was going to put the fire out.
His body was burned beyond recognition. The two boys
were asphyxiated. They had no marks on them other than
some of the carbon particles. Both kids, one in one room
under a bed, and the other one in a corner of another room,
were found trying to claw their way out. We had total frustration that night. After the mother got off work, she went
out with some guy and came back about 9:00 A.M. I had a
difficult time feeling any compassion for that woman.

Another time we had two little black kids who died in
a fire. These kids, by the way—and adults will do the same
thing—got in a prenatal position. They'll go into a closet,
they'll go behind a chair, they'll go behind furniture, and
they'll get in a prenatal position. That's the way we find
them. The kids were right by a bedroom window. All they
had to do was open that bedroom window, but nobody
ever told them of an alternate escape route. One of our
paramedics went in and found both the kids and brought
them out, but they were both killed. The mother had been
at a bar and left the two kids by themselves.

Q: And your feeling, Chief, was one of frustration?
A: One of frustration that these kids were probably alive at
     the time we pulled up except that we didn't know that.

What bothered me is that I had gone right by that window. I was truck company captain at the time. I had gone right by that window, but we had to go through the house and go through normal search patterns. By the time we got to the back room, those kids had expired.

Chapter Eleven

TO CATCH AN ARSONIST

The owner of a home destroyed by an explosion and fire that killed two men has been booked for investigation of murder and arson, investigators said. Meanwhile, the teenagers whose charred bodies were found in the kitchen of the home early Thursday have been identified as Paul Cort, 17, and Tom Stone, 16, both of Lorel City.

"Terry Polk," 29, was arrested in Los Angeles, a few blocks from where he worked at a service station owned by his brother. He remained in County jail pending his expected arraignment Tuesday, the Fire Captain said.

Arson investigators found a "whole lot" of evidence pointing to Polk. Said one investigator, "It was no one particular thing. Just a lot of good, hard work." This investigator alleged that collecting insurance was the motive for the deliberately set blaze that ripped off the house's roof and rocked the southeastern Lorel City neighborhood but caused no damage to other homes. A 5-gallon can of flammable liquid was found at the demolished home.

Polk said that he was working at his brother's service station when the explosion occurred. He said he had given no one permission to enter the vacant house. He had moved out of the house several months ago, but would return on weekends, a Fire Department spokesman said. The two juveniles killed in the incident were described by authorities as "trying to do a job."[1]

A state reward was posted Monday for an arsonist who started a fire that burned through 400 acres of grass, at least four century-old homes and a historic ferry boat. "We're calling it arson, with at least eight original fires set

in the same period of time and roughly the same location,"
Forestry Battalion Chief Carl Wirst said. "It doesn't look
like it could be anything else."

The state posted reward bulletins in the area, offering
$5,000 for information leading to an arrest in the fire. The
fire broke out Sunday afternoon and was controlled Monday morning.

"It was awesome. In 25 years of firefighting I've never
seen anything like it," Bud Oles of the Camel Fire Department said. Several fire fighters were overcome by
smoke but there were no other injuries. About 300 volunteers joined fire fighters and even used buckets and garden hoses to fight the flames.[2]

While riding on a bike with a friend during a lunch
break from Sierra High School, a fifteen-year-old boy
named Arnold Best tossed a simple cigarette device into
the brush at the side of Canyon Road. Although Arnold
reportedly attempted to stop the spread of his little fire
when he saw it getting out of hand, neither he nor the 500
or more fire fighters who eventually responded had much
luck. When the flames finally lost their momentum at the
beach in Santa Monica, they'd razed 130 homes, 121 other
structures and 21 mobile homes.

At least three people were seriously injured and a
dozen more hospitalized with less severe burns and
wounds. When searchers found the body of Bill Small, a
67-year-old resident who'd been overrun by the fire while
taking his daily hike, arson investigators turned the case
over to the Los Angeles County sheriff's Homicide Division.

According to Detective Sam Pearson, the primary investigator on the case, two years of "a lot of legwork and
a lot of sifting"—including hundreds of interviews with
residents of the area and Sierra High School students—
convinced investigators that they had enough evidence to
bring charges against the firesetter. Arnold, then 17-years-
old, was found guilty of second-degree murder and felony

brush burning. He was sentenced to serve three years behind bars with the California Youth Authority.[3]

The most effective method of detecting arson clearly would be to examine every fire. This procedure is used in some cities, but for most communities, the costs are unacceptably high. More typically, the arson squad is called in to investigate only when the battalion chief identifies the fire as suspicious in origin.

Another method of selecting cases for fire investigation is to establish external criteria, such as the seriousness of the fire, any loss of life or injury to civilians or fire fighters, or fires with high monetary loss. By setting such "fire seriousness" criteria, the department knows that the number of its arson investigations will match both the financial resources available for fire investigations and the investigative capacity of the arson unit.[4]

Because of these restrictions, many fires unfortunately receive only a perfunctory investigation, and many others are not investigated at all. This is true both in the initial investigation to find out if the fire is of arson origin and in the subsequent criminal investigation when arson has actually been determined.

In a 1975 study in New Jersey, the Arson Investigation Bureau of the National Institute of Law Enforcement and Criminal Justice reported that only 16,221 of 72,736 fires (22 percent) in the state had been investigated. Further, of the 31,541 fires for that year that were declared to be actual arson, or to be of a suspicious or undetermined nature, just a few over half were investigated.[5]

Expressing concern, the Arson Investigation Bureau noted, by way of comparison, the large investigative effort given to bank robberies by both the FBI and local police, even when there have been considerably fewer bank holdups than serious fires. In 1974, for example, the actual number of bank robberies in the United States was 3,500, and the total dollar loss was $13 million. By contrast, the national figures for arson fires for that same year was 187,000 for a total loss of $616 million.[6]

This low rate of fire investigation is due to two primary factors: one stems from the physical nature of fire scenes; the other arises from administrative problems.

According to the FBI, no other type of crime scene except bombing is characterized by as much disorder and destruction as arson. The arson investigator must often search through rubble for clues; the presence of water and foam remaining from extinguishing the fire further impedes the search; moreover, the scene is often dangerous to work in; and the fire suppression and mop-up often further destroy clues. It is no wonder with obstacles such as these that many fires are never investigated.

The administrative problem is often one of jurisdiction. Historically, the police have viewed arson as a fire problem, but fire fighters argue that it is a police problem because fire fighters are not trained investigators. Smaller communities that do not have special arson investigation units usually allocate to the fire departments the responsibility for investigating the causes of fires and for arson detection, and the law-enforcement agencies are charged with the responsibility for criminal investigation and the apprehension of a suspect.[7]

The first step in a fire investigation is for the investigator to confer with fire fighters on the scene to find out about smoke color, odor, size of flame, and other important information that cannot be discovered after the fire is out. Those fire fighters who arrive first on the scene are expected to recall the number of separate fires, the intensity and speed of the fire, and the behavior of persons near the fire. Other items to investigate in determining arson are the presence of foreign materials that could accelerate the fire's speed, open doors and windows that might provide ventilation, inoperative sprinklers and fire doors, and tracks and footprints.

The investigator also documents the arson scene through photographs, written reports of what was seen, measurements, and sketches. With this information, the investigator reconstructs the sequence of the fire back to its origin. Arsonists often use "trailers" (connecting devices) between fires, chemicals or flammable liquids, timing devices, electrical equipment, and firebombs. By focusing on the incendiary device, the investigator can tell how, and possibly why, the fire occurred.[8]

Once it has been determined that a fire was of incendiary origin, the investigator must discover the motive. As we have documented, there are many different and complex motives for firesetting. According to investigators, however, the single most common motive for arson fires set by adults is insurance fraud. Furthermore, as the first newspaper account presented at the beginning of this chapter demonstrates, on occasion juveniles are hired by adults to spark these fires.

In residential and business fires where fraud is suspected, investigators look for specific clues to indicate intent. In residential fires, for example, items having sentimental value (photographs, antiques) or high monetary value (cash, stocks) are usually removed before the fire is ignited. Clothing or furnishings are often removed or replaced with cheap goods before the fire. Investigators also determine, if family pets survived the fire, whether they were released prior to the fire or escaped during it.[9]

In the case of fires set by juveniles, investigators can easily determine those caused by a child from the amount of evidence left lying around. In both "playing-with-matches" fires and "crying-for-help" fires, there are clearcut signs to aid the investigative staff, such as the location of the fires, the incendiary device, and the child's admission of guilt. With the older juvenile firesetters, and with "delinquent" fires and fires set by "severely disturbed" juveniles, the arson investigators must often use more sophisticated techniques. These investigations are similar to those conducted on fires set by adult arsonists and professional torches.

One investigative technique found to be useful in determining that a fire was set by a juvenile gang is "pattern recognition," which was first employed in 1975 in Maryland. The fire department investigative unit coded all fires in terms of the date of the incident, the location, the type of fire, the time the alarm was received, the day of the week, and the number of alarms. By looking at these coded fires over time, the arson investigators noted distinct patterns in terms of location and time. With this information, they were able to watch and arrest the gang members when the coded pattern indicated that the times of the multiple fires corresponded repeatedly with breaks in the school day.[10] This technique of pattern recognition is now widely used.

Even with such investigative successes, more needs to be done. According to a study of 27 arson investigators (of some 6,000 in the nation), eight critical needs were expressed. In decreasing order of priority, these needs included: increased training; more arson investigators; a computerized arson-investigation data system; scientific research; cooperation from insurance companies; technological developments; clarified jurisdiction over arson cases; and increased availability of crime laboratories.[11]

To gain additional information on arson investigation procedures and cases dealing with juveniles, we interviewed two investigators of a large metropolitan fire department in Los Angeles County:

Q: What is the procedure by which you are called in on a case?
A: The battalion chief calls for us in all fires of suspicious or-
     igin. The actual requirement is to bring us in on every fire
     with over $3,000 damage, of suspicious origin, or when
     there is an injury or death to a civilian or a fire fighter. The
     two of us work a rotation shift, with one of us always on
     duty. At home they can reach us by beeper when we are
     on call.

Q: How many cases per year do you work on? What percentage
     of these are juvenile arson cases?
A: We had 241 arson cases last year. We are terribly under-
     staffed. We actually now have a case load for eight inves-
     tigators. Of the total, 10 percent to 15 percent are juvenile
     arson cases.

Q: How long does it take to crack a case?
A: Usually it takes about three hours at the fire scene to com-
     plete the initial investigation. Then, we have to work on
     suspect development and background investigation. We
     are authorized to handle all the evidence and follow the
     case through to court sentencing. In terms of the actual
     arrest of the offender, this varies from "nailing the mutt"
     at the scene to obtaining a breakthrough some months later.
     Usually, however, if we don't get something in the first few
     days, the case is dropped because we are overworked and
     don't have time. The first few days are critical.
        We have had this arson investigaton unit in the city
     since 1973, when we took it over from the police depart-
     ment. We have excellent rapport with other city and county
     agencies.

Q: Any distinctive features about juvenile arson cases?
A: Yeah, they are stupid in the mechanics of setting the fire.
     Also, where they set fires. With fires at school, they are
     either seen committing the arson, or they brag about it to
     their friends, who then turn them in. Most juveniles don't
     try to cover up the arson. They are not as professional or
     mature as adults. Their method of operation is not that
     great. But sometimes their fires are very effective without
     their actually knowing much about what they are doing.

Q: What types of fires do juveniles set in this city?

A: Trash cans, vacant garages, Christmas trees, palm trees, and schools.

Q: How serious have the school fires been?

A: In one stretch of four years, we solved six out of the seven school fires. We haven't had a decent school fire in some time. Last spring, however, we had a fire at Montgomery High School. Three fires were set at the same time in three separate locations. One of the fires was in a classroom in the middle of the building. We have fifteen suspects. It seems that the teacher had handed out fifteen failing notices approximately twelve hours before the fires. Not only were the three fires set, but they deliberately opened up her drawer and tore her husband's picture in half, lit it on fire, and then shoved it back in the drawer. Without oxygen, this fire went out, but not before part of the picture had burned.

     Because of the nature of the fires, we perceived that one or more of the kids was angered by failing. It was a tenth-grade class, and so we are in the process of getting fingerprints of all fifteen kids to compare them with the prints taken at the fire scene. The other fires included setting papers on fire in one section of the room and setting test papers on fire on a classroom table.

     We have had fewer school fires than in the past because of the fire alarm system. All schools now have smoke detection systems and intrusion sounding devices [for break-ins]. So now the fire is either detected earlier or the would-be arsonist is apprehended before any major fire damage can take place.

Q: What type of fires are more frequently set by juveniles?

A: The "burg and burn" type [burglary and burn]. It's becoming more prevalent for all age groups because of the fingerprinting factor. They think that by setting a fire after they have burglarized a place, the fire department will come in and spray water and conceal their entry.

Q: What have been some of your distinctive arson cases involving juveniles?

A: We've had several. One old case was Roy Jones, which began in 1974 and lasted for several years. It started with a garage fire of suspicious origin near where there had been a series of recent fires. One investigator saw him at the site of a nearby trash fire two weeks later, and then we began noticing him, too. However, we had nothing to nail him on.

He turned out to be a true pyromaniac. When we finally apprehended him, he had set over 250 fires, and we charged him with eight counts of arson. He knew every fire station in the area by zone. He would call in a false alarm—or have one of his buddies call in the alarm—to a particular zone, which would tie up the fire department in a direction different from where he would then set his fires. In his bedroom, we found a giant map on which he had preplanned the exact routes that the various fire trucks would take.

We spent 1½ years before we got him. What finally caught him was he had been going with this gal who was older than he was. She was forty and Roy was nineteen; she was a mother figure to him. He was sexually frustrated, and he would beat the shit out of her. She snitched him off and set him up. My investigative partner at the time had also gone under cover and went to some of his parties to get him.

He's from England and they were going to deport him. But while he was in jail he married an American, and so they couldn't deport him. He served 2½ years.

My most frustrating case involved a fourteen-year-old kid who had set a quarter-million-dollar fire in a navy housing area. I worked with navy intelligence, and we tracked this kid down, convicted him, only to have a "juvenile referee judge" only place him on probation. It seems that the judge felt sorry for the kid because on the day of arraignment, the kid's dog had died.

Most kids who set fires are from separated or divorced families. One thirteen-year-old set a community church on fire every Tuesday or Thursday. We caught him on the fourth fire because he was always in the crowd at the fire and because he was always asking a lot of questions. His big thing was blacks had made him do it. His mom was white; his mom's boyfriend was Mexican.

In one of our biggest fires, we arrested a sixteen-year-old known burglar who had taken a stereo home from a fire that destroyed a grocery store, a liquor market, and a laundromat. New owners had recently bought the complex and were going to tear it down to build offices. The boy claimed that he had been paid to set the fire but didn't know who really paid him. The boy was sent to jail but we couldn't arrest the owners because we couldn't prove they were involved.

It seems that adults are more regular in their firesetting. With adults, it is a "Wednesday-night-off-and-nothing-to-do" type of thing. Kids are more random. Except for Christmas time. Kids love to burn those discarded Christmas trees. One kid placed a bunch of trees in an enclosed trash area and set them on fire, which then spread and destroyed the entire carport in the apartment building, four cars, and a boat.

Another interesting case was the seventeen-year-old juvenile with a high IQ who made a smoke bomb. He got two other kids to help him—one of these kids was the son of a fire captain—and they placed the smoke bomb in the school auditorium while two thousand or so students were watching a school play. It was meant as a kind of prank. The boys did not realize the likelihood of panic, and as the juvenile who made the bomb said when interviewed by the investigators on video, "My friends are agile enough; they can get out." The bomb had been made from material taken from the chemistry lab.

Q: What special training did you get as arson investigators?
A: Much of our training is on the job. We attend workshops and seminars. To be qualified as an "expert witness," we attended the National Fire Academy for two weeks, where we had to pass tests to be certified. Because we are the only

ones in the fire department to attend the police academy, we can, and do, carry a gun. The fire department has arrest power at a fire scene only—citizen's arrest. Arson investigators have arrest powers throughout the state.

Arson investigation has become sophisticated only since the early 1970s. Arson still has a low priority even though it is now a Type I crime. Someone goes and does a burglary or gets a hundred dollars from an armed bank robbery, and it's on the evening news. But with most fires, it's never covered, even when the damage is greater.

With the public, there is the attitude of "not to worry" [about the fire] because they know that the insurance will pay for it. With the fire insurance commercials on television, the people get paid right away. [Some insurance companies like the big fires because the insurance company gets publicity and people buy more insurance.]

Q: What is your working relationship with the other protection agencies?

A: We are teased a lot by the other fire fighters for actually being cops. But we have excellent rapport with both departments. Because of this, we get full cooperation, and the fire fighters help out by not destroying evidence until we get there. We have been lucky because other investigators, not as well liked, sometimes don't get the cooperation.

Q: What further work do you have to do once a juvenile is apprehended? What type of arrest rates do you have?

A: Three-quarters of our time is involved with paperwork and court appearances. Our success rate is high because we only choose the "viable" cases that we feel are workable and are likely to lead to a conviction. Close to 80 percent of the cases we decide to work on lead to an arrest, and 99.9 percent of these result in our filing a petition [charge] against the offender. With only two investigators, we can't waste time. With eight investigators, we could accept more cases and quadruple our arrests.

One innovative technique we use is to videotape our interviews with witnesses, victims, and suspects. We show these tapes to the district attorney and the courts. With kids under fourteen years of age, we have to do a "Gladys R."—twenty questions that determine whether the child understands the difference between right and wrong and understands his or her right to remain silent. With kids over fourteen, we just have to read them their rights. The tapes give us visual evidence on each case, and so the prosecuting attorneys don't even "chip teeth" [argue] with us anymore. Most people whom we arrest talk to us and admit the fires.

Arson investigators are not the only ones apprehending firesetters these days. Increasingly, the public is becoming involved in arson prevention and intervention:

The woman leaning out of the window to get a breath of air was only mildly curious at the surreptitious activity in the shop across the street. It wasn't until the flames erupted—hours later—that she made the connection.

The loss was substantial. The fire had spread to neighboring businesses, too. Still the woman did not come forward. It was pretty obvious that the man she had seen—and could probably recognize if she saw him again—had played a role in the fire. But women looking out of windows do not want to mess around with arsonists—lest they wake up some night burning up in their own bed.

It wasn't until she spotted the red and white poster tacked to a pole in the vicinity of the fire that she decided to tell what she knew. It promised her complete anonymity. She wouldn't even have to give her name. And if the information led to the arrest and conviction of the arsonist, she could even stand to gain up to $500 as a reward. She went to a telephone booth and called the toll-free number listed on the poster.

The operator who answered was skilled at drawing out the key points of the information she had to offer. And he didn't ask for her name. Instead, he gave her a code name and a case number with which she might later claim her reward if her information proved to be of value. It was one more success story in a statewide network designed to provide the most devastating tool with which society can protect itself from the arsonist—a witness.[12]

Begun in the State of California in 1971, "We TIP," standing for "We Turn in Pushers," first involved the community in curbing the drug problem by setting up a reward system of up to five hundred dollars for anonymous information that would assist investigators in the arrest and conviction of drug criminals. The program was so successful that it was expanded into all major crime areas, including arson.

In the Los Angeles County area, the We TIP's "War On Arson" has been in operation since 1979. With a working staff of eight, the program is totally nonprofit and relies on public donations. The procedures followed when a witness calls in are standard and are similar to those illustrated in the above newspaper account. The We TIP information is considered an investigative tool only. Informants cannot testify in court and also remain anonymous. The information they provide can only guide the investigators in the proper direction.[13]

According to San Bernardino County figures, during the year 1981 We TIP received over six hundred anonymous tips related to crime in the county, ranging through arson, drugs, burglary, robbery, and assault. These tips aided in over 150 arrests and convictions, as well as the closing of many cases by investigating law-enforcement agencies. In 1980, the conviction rate of those arrested as a result of calls to We TIP stood at 42 percent. In 1981, the conviction rate had risen to 63 percent.[14]

The We TIP organization now actively advertises its service by placing posters at the scenes of fires of suspicious origin, by placing newspaper ads, and by running public service announcements explaining the program on radio and television.

Other community prevention measures employed to deter arson behavior are the presence of police and/or fire department suppression-units that patrol those neighborhoods with high arson activity. The officers are visible at high-incidence times of the day in areas where suspicious fires have been set. They converse with merchants and residents, explaining their presence and requesting assistance with information on arson fires. These programs have received tremendous community support. Similar programs have been proposed in other states, as they appear to be effective in curbing juvenile arson and vandalism.

Chapter Twelve

TREATMENT OF THE OFFENDER

Many newly opened treatment programs aimed at assisting both the younger, less serious fire offender and the older, more serious juvenile arsonist are being developed. These treatment programs vary in approach from administering aversion therapy and behavioral modification to matching young firesetters with volunteer fire fighters, as in the Catholic Big Brothers Organization. Innovative therapeutic strategies are being used as well in hospital settings.

As we have noted in previous chapters, the Fire Intervention Program of the San Bernardino County Probation Department incorporated, and expanded on, the programs suggested by the classification manual developed for the U.S. Fire Administration. This manual, in fact, has served as the framework for fire safety programs that have been recently developed in other cities and counties throughout California, as well as across the nation and abroad.

These community-based programs are generally set up to assist the young, first-time offender, whereas the older, recidivist juvenile offender is more often treated in controlled facilities such as hospitals or state correctional facilities. To date, the government manual has developed procedures to be followed in working with the juvenile arsonist under eight years old and from eight to fourteen years old. In the future, procedures will be available that offer suggestions for working with the older teenage firesetter. The merit of this manual lies in its not only providing fire personnel, probation officers, psychologists, and counselors with means of measuring the severity of the child's problem with fire, but in its also providing them with strategies for fire safety intervention for each specific and corresponding level of severity. These detailed strategies, with some modification and elaboration, were used in the San Bernardino fire-safety program and were administered to the firesetters in our sample group.

The primary goal of all the fire-safety programs, obviously, is to correct the juvenile's firesetting behavior. Moreover, the younger the child, the greater is the active cooperation required from the parents. For example, with the very young child who is preverbal and has limited understanding, parents must be made responsible for prevention by emphatically warning the child *not* to play with fire and by keeping ignition sources away from the child. Appropriate educational pamphlets to use with this younger child (under age three) are available to parents, as a community service, through most fire departments.

For the "playing-with-matches" and some "crying-for-help" firesetters, who possess some understanding, the fire-safety manual suggests several approaches to reinforcing the proper use of fire: educational programs, aversion therapy, and behavioral modification, which were incorporated into the San Bernardino County Fire Intervention Program.

The most common treatment with the younger juvenile firesetter is the *educational program*. The strategy draws on a variety of approaches. One approach is to develop a series of questions to ask the younger child: how to help people not to get hurt by fire; how to differentiate between when such items such as matches, birthday candles, a kitchen stove, and an electrical cord can be helpful, and when they can be hazardous; and what the child should do in case of fire. Another technique is to give the younger child a paper assignment such as coloring in green the good fire-safety habits in a picture of a house, and coloring in red the fire safety hazards in the house. Or the child is instructed to connect the dots in a picture that concludes with the child in the drawing finding the best way to get out of a smoke-filled room.

A second educational approach is to show the child appropriate teaching films about fire, including films showing the danger to fire fighters. It is specifically recommended that photographs and films showing burn victims *not* be shown to young children because, according to the manual, such films merely scare them and do not reinforce a positive learning experience.

A third educational approach is to involve the child in being responsible for his or her fire safety and to encourage him or her to help prevent fires at home. The manual suggests that the child promise to use matches only under the supervision of an adult, and to explain why it is inappropriate for the child to play with matches. The child should also be encouraged to inform adult authorities if other children are playing with fire. Fire prevention tasks such as emptying dirty ashtrays are also recommended for the youngster under age eight.

More specific examples were developed by the San Bernardino staff. One educational technique is to give the young child a series of drawings to color, including a picture of a young boy throwing a bucket of water on a burning campfire and a picture of a Bambi-like deer caught in a forest fire. Another technique is to ask the child to develop a series of questions that one might ask fire fighters so that the child would learn about their important job of protecting people from fire. Another assignment includes a checklist of home fire-safety precautions, which the child completes with the assistance of her or his parents, so that they all share in the concern. The clinical psychologists also ask children to draw a series of pictures involving themselves and their family, and themselves with fire. These drawings are then discussed with the child so that feelings concerning family issues and fire play can be addressed. The county has also developed an individualized self-learning program in fire prevention that children are assigned to complete and turn in to their probation officers.

With the older (eight- to fourteen-year-old) juvenile, more sophisticated educational strategies are recommended. The older elementary- and junior-high-school-aged "crying-for-help" and "delinquent" firesetters are assigned such tasks as writing an essay on ten incidents that cause burns and how to correct the incidents and treat the burns; interviewing a fire fighter and writing an essay on the tasks she or he performs; reading the section on fire in a Boy Scout manual and completing the badge exercises, which include learning proper fire-building methods and how correctly to extinguish campfires; and making and displaying a fire-safety poster.

Fire prevention and safety tests have also been developed for preteenage firesetters. One test for this age group asks them to study proper fire-safety measures and then answer twenty-five questions of moderate difficulty, such as: what should one do if one's clothes catch on fire; what should one do if there is a fire in the oven; what should one do for minor burns; and which one of several fabrics is most difficult to ignite and burn? (For those readers who would like to take this test, the twenty-five questions for the "Learn Not to Burn" Knowledge Test published by the National Fire Protection Association, along with the answers, are in Appendix C.)

Another technique used with the younger firesetters is *aversion therapy*. This negative-practice strategy is suggested when working with youngsters who "play with matches." The philosophy behind this approach is to allow the child to light so many matches, under parental supervision, that he or she becomes saturated and bored by the process and develops an aversion to fire play. In the San Bernardino Fire Safety Program, some probation officers include, as part of the juvenile's "Home Fire Prevention Course," the assignment of having to light 200 matches, one by one, in a safe place (such as the driveway), in a properly prescribed manner, and under adult supervision. When questioned about whether such an approach would actually deter a child from lighting a fire ever again, the probation officers contend that the approach does work with some children.

With at least one preteenager in the San Bernardino group, this approach apparently did work. In a letter written to his probation officer, the boy explained that he had "learned his lesson," as the following account shows:

> I have finished the tasks you gave me and I made, lit, smuthered [sic], stamped, and watered a box fire and teepee fire in my back yard. I hope I have done a good job for you and please write me and tell [me] if I have done a good job. I have learned my lesson and I won't do that again. That's all I can say is I won't do it again. I promise that. I will try not to do it again. My hand is sore. I probably can't write for a week.

Another common technique used with these youngsters is *behavioral modification*. Rather than using negative conditioning, as in aversion therapy, this approach rewards positive behavior and encourages the youngster to understand the motivations behind his or her past firesetting behavior. With this understanding and insight, the youngster is then rewarded for responding to stress events in appropriate and socially approved ways rather than in antisocial and socially unapproved ways, such as firesetting.

One hospital has combined two of the three approaches—fire-safety education and behavioral modification—in treating the more serious juvenile firesetter. In a letter to one of the fire-safety counselors in our San Bernardino group, this treatment hospital in Portland, Oregon, explained their Juvenile Firesetters Program:

> The majority of your questions centered around our use of the "firesetting test": allowing the child to set a fire in a controlled environment. There are several steps that precede this test. First, we gather all of the information we can about the child and about his firesetting behavior from the child, from his parents, and from others in the community (i.e., the school or other referring agency). Then we observe the child for a period of time as he goes through the structured activities in the hospital. At this same time, we also do psychological, physical, educational, neurological, social, and whatever other evaluations seem appropriate. Finally, when we have gathered as many data as we can about the child and can make some fairly accurate predictions about what moods would induce firesetting behavior, the child's therapist attempts to reproduce that mood. The child is then placed in an enclosed, fairly fireproof patio, where he has a choice of play materials. Secreted in those materials are matches and lighters. He is carefully monitored for attempts to use those matches and lighters. Afterward, he is "debriefed" and asked about the feelings he had as he found the matches, and as he perhaps attempted to light a fire. When it seems appropriate, this test is moved to the child's bedroom, to the hospital grounds, or to places in the community such as parks. The hope, of course, is that the child will learn to identify which moods lead him to set fires and that he will learn alternate ways of working through those moods.

So far, all of our firesetting children have appeared to be clinically depressed, and this test was developed primarily with that kind of child. It works for us because we have enough carefully trained staff to support the observations, because we have the child with us long enough to be able to make enough observations, and because we have a facility that provides a safe, easily monitored area in which to make this test. We would hesitate to recommend such a test to anyone who could not meet these criteria.

The program itself has two other components. The first is family treatment. Whenever it is possible, we involve the parents in family therapy, either with the child's primary therapist or with the hospital's family therapist. When it is appropriate, we also involve the parents in parenting classes taught here at the hospital. The parents need to understand the child's behavior and to be as involved in his therapy as possible. This is a standard part of our child and adolescent program.

The final component of the Juvenile Firesetters Program is that of community treatment. We find ourselves involved in educating referral agencies about the causes and identification of problem juvenile firesetting and have been involved in teaching a number of seminars. We also work closely with schools and other community agencies that may be involved with a particular child. We try to set up appropriate support systems and to follow up therapy for the child when he leaves our program, and we will continue to consult with those agencies on an as-needed basis following the child's discharge from our program.[1]

A new and exciting treatment program is the community-based Firehawk program begun in 1981 in San Francisco. This approach brings young firesetters together with fire fighters on a one-to-one basis. It has been so successful that it has matured into the National Firehawk Foundation, with programs in twenty-two states.

The focus of the program, in effect, is to have the fire fighters serve as parent substitutes for those children who often set fires as a means of gaining attention or because they are lonely. The point of the program is not to punish the child but, instead, to assist the child in developing a responsible attitude toward fire and an appreciation of the work that fire fighters do in putting out fires. The fire fighters who volunteer for the program undergo three training sessions before they are paired with children, and the director of the program matches a child and a fire fighter who will be compatible. According to this official, the program, in its initial years, has been a success. None of the twenty youths originally selected for the program has returned to setting fires—a 100 percent "nonrekindling" rate. And an additional 160 youths who were involved in the program on a short-term or one-time basis have also not resumed arson behavior.[2]

We would suspect that, with proper screening, a program such as this Firehawk approach would benefit our three lesser categories of juvenile firesetters. As can be seen, both the therapeutic programs and the other treatment programs, such as the "big brother" approach, can assist worried parents with their firesetting youngsters. And these varied approaches all require the combined and concerted efforts of the parents and fire-safety personnel in assisting the juvenile offender to gain a proper respect for fire.

A more structured program has been developed in Ohio for "delinquent" firesetters. Housed in one state facility, the convicted arsonists—in groups numbering five to eight youths at a time—are assigned to a twelve-week course that meets three hours per week. The classes involve a variety of educational activities, including films on fire safety and the role of fire fighters, supervised fieldtrips to the fire academy (where recruits are trained in becoming fire fighters) and a fire department, a visit to the burn ward of a child's hospital, and periodic exams. Toward the end of the course, the wards present a fire-safety program to an assembly of persons, including staff members and any parents who are able to attend. On graduation day, at the end of the twelve weeks, a slide show is presented showing the wards' activities and accomplishments.

Because our study employs the classification manual's behavioral characteristics, we decided to interview Dr. Kenneth R. Fineman, the chief architect of the manual, and ask him to comment on some questions raised from the findings in our study:

Q: How widely used is the classification manual?

A: It is now being used in some thirty states. Although it was primarily aimed at fire departments, its usage has spread to probation officers, counselors, and juvenile justice people in general. Mental health personnel are also using the manual.

Q: What behavioral characteristics did you feel would be the strongest indicators of firesetters as opposed to nonfiresetters?

A: The child's family relationship. We felt that it would be those indicators that showed that the parents had been unable to deal adequately with the child. As a clinical psychologist working with juvenile firesetters and their families, I have found that these juveniles come from single-parent homes. And if their father is present, he remains aloof and difficult—often not participating in the therapeutic sessions. These fathers have a "macho" image that cuts across socioeconomic lines.

With the firesetters themselves, we feel that they have school problems and peer group difficulties. We also believe that there is a subgroup of more classically delinquent juveniles.

Q: What behavioral characteristics did you feel would differentiate the younger firesetters from the older ones?

A: With kids under seven, we feel that their setting fires is due to family stress and the home environment. With the latency-age kids (eight to thirteen), we feel there are also family-related problems. In this sense, these kids are similar to the younger ones. However, the more disturbed kids are also in this age category. Also, a subgroup of this age group are precocious like the older juveniles, and they're concerned about the attention from their peer group. With the older kids, firesetting may also be caused by an overreaction from a putdown by school authorities. Also, there is the ingestion of drugs and alcohol with teenagers.

Q: What is the therapeutic strategy that you advise one to employ with the different ages of firesetters?

A: With younger kids, therapy should be very behavioral-oriented. For instance, you set up structured systems in their home—that is, a token economy with parents in control of rewarding the child for positive behavior. The therapist also plays the role of the rewarder. The goal in therapy is always to suppress the firesetting behavior immediately because it is potentially so dangerous. With this behavioral approach, it is important to involve the parents in the therapy. All the families of firesetters, and particularly the women who are single parents, are quite "field-dependent." They need more structure from their external environment. And the behavioral approach, under the direction of the therapist, provides the family with this structure.

   With the older kids, you take a more psychodynamic point of view. Therapy focuses on the reasons for and the patterns of their firesetting behavior.

Q: Is juvenile firesetting on the increase?

A: It appears that, in those parts of the country where there is no fire-safety program, fires are definitely increasing. It would be surprising to see if there is a statistically significant decrease in juvenile firesetting. As firesetting behavior becomes more identified and techniques in detecting arson

improve, the incidences of actual juvenile arsonists will
very likely increase. It would be nice if the actual number
is going down. However, I do not think this is the case.

Q: Have any foreign countries indicated an interest in your
classification manual?

A: The countries that seem to be most interested in our program include England, Germany, Holland, Poland, and
Japan.

Q: What is your "pet theory" as to why these kids set fires?

A: Fire for these kids is a function of sensory deprivation.
When early family bonding is absent—the positive warmth
and cuddling exchanges between mother and child—fire
can become a compensation for such deprivation.

Q: Why fire?

A: Because it exists; it is present and available; and it is com-
pensatory. With such early sensory deprivation, the child
is at risk at an early age, and the deprivation leads to a need
for a severe stimulus, which fire provides.

Q: How was the classification manual developed?

A: We first reviewed every article in the field. I began working
on it in 1975 and then founded the Fire Services Committee,
which developed a prospectus that was submitted to the
government, approved, and funded. We field-tested the
manual for a year.

So far, we have discussed the treatment programs
available to the young, less serious offender. But as we
pointed out in Chapter 9, the older, more serious juvenile
offender is less likely to be treated in community diversion
programs such as we have presented here. Instead, the
more serious "delinquent" and "severely disturbed" juvenile arsonists are sentenced to correctional facilities,
where they are treated within the correctional facilities
under the auspices of the California Youth Authority.

Within the Youth Authority itself, there are a variety
of programs, including two reception centers, schools, and

camps. The reception centers—one in the northern part of the state and one in the southern part—are the facilities where much of the diagnostic testing and treatment take place. Once a ward is deemed psychologically suitable for placement among the other wards, she or he is reassigned to another correctional institution or is moved from the psychiatric wing to another section or wing of that facility.

Because arsonists who are committed to the Youth Authority are often the most dangerous type of firesetter, they are treated—along with the equally dangerous rapists and child molesters—in one of two special programs that the Youth Authority has developed. Both these programs—the Intensive Treatment Program (ITP) and the Special Counseling Program (SCP), begun in 1979, assist those wards who have not been able to adapt to the average Youth Authority programs and who require special care because of their serious mental, emotional, and social problems.

According to the state officials we interviewed, the basic difference between these two clinical programs is the therapeutic approach that is used and the different staffing. In the Intensive Treatment Program, treatment is given to the more psychotic, severely neurotic, and even borderline schizophrenic juvenile by a team of psychiatrists who employ a variety of therapeutic techniques, including neo-Freudian psychoanalysis, small group transactional analysis, and one-on-one therapy. The Special Counseling Program, on the other hand, treats the more psychopathic and antisocial juvenile by using a variety of approaches, including behavioral modification, which focuses on problem-oriented and goal-and-skill–oriented therapy; assertiveness training; anger management; and group therapy. This program is administered by both trained clinical psychologists and probation workers. Thus, the ITP uses the medical model approach and is administered by psychiatrists, whereas the SCP uses the behavioral-modification approach and is administered by psychologists and probation personnel.

According to state officials, the Youth Authority has attempted some innovative treatment programs in the past. One such program was the Fricot Ranch experiment in 1965, which studied the outcome of small versus large living groups in the rehabilitation of delinquents who had committed various crimes. Those juveniles who were housed in the smaller, twenty-bed facilities were found to receive five times more staff attention than the control subjects, who were housed in the larger, fifty-bed facilities. The study supported the belief that rehabilitation can be better accomplished in small living units, where the higher staff-to-ward ratios provide more opportunities for both formal and informal interaction.[3]

What makes this Fricot Ranch project of interest to our study is that in 1980, a fifteen-year follow-up study was conducted that looked at the adult "criminal careers" of these former juvenile offenders. As it happened, nearly one-fourth of those juveniles randomly selected for inclusion in the 1965 group had a firesetting offense. In the follow-up study, those with arson backgrounds who had been housed in the smaller living groups had a *lower* overall recidivist crime rate than those who had initially committed certain other offenses, and than those who had been housed in the larger living units. Further, those wards, including many of the firesetters, who had originally been classified as neurotics appeared to have benefited from the more individualized attention of this intensive program.[4]

Further long-term comparative research is needed to clarify in what ways early therapeutic intervention—and smaller one-to-one interaction—with juvenile arsonists *does* decrease the level of recidivism and why these kinds of programs are more successful with young arsonists than with those who are apprehended for other types of crime. We would contend that the lower recidivism rates of juvenile arsonists who receive therapy are due in part to the passive-aggressive nature of their earlier behavior. As the hospital program in Oregon noted, juveniles can be assisted, step by step, to develop appropriate responses to stressful situations and can learn to control their firesetting "urges." With appropriate therapeutic intervention, many of the less and moderately severe firesetters can be rehabilitated.

With the more severe, and psychotic, firesetters, however, the chances for complete rehabilitation are problematic. We were able to interview the treatment director of one of the three Intensive Treatment Programs who works specifically with the most severe juvenile firesetters housed in the California Youth Authority:

Q: Can you discuss any general patterns among the firesetters you have worked with?

A: We have treated a variety of boys here. Some boys have even deliberately set themselves on fire. Usually, firesetters who are suicidal harm themselves in other ways, such as cutting themselves. We have treated those with psychotic hallucinations who claim that voices told them to set the fires. And we have treated those with character disorders, who are younger than the psychotics when they begin to set their fires.

In general, those juveniles who set fires early are often quite severe. The pattern appears to be firesetting, torturing animals, and then going on to more violent aggressive acts, such as rape, murder, and child molestation.

I am currently treating a fifteen-year-old Chicano boy who is here for attempted murder. He had stabbed someone over thirty times. The year before this incident, he had been on probation for having set fire to a lumber yard with a $1-million loss. He had also tortured a dog and had sodomized his eight-year-old brother on many occasions over a two-year period.

Another boy, seventeen, was caught setting fire to the car of a fire chief. He had been abandoned often by his mother and was living in a foster home at the time of this fire. He had a history of firesetting, beginning with setting his mother's bed sheets on fire when he was five. Kids such as this boy who are vengeful and malicious often have a history of setting fires that attack the nurturing environment of the home. One boy, for example, would burglarize a home, have a bowel movement somewhere in the house, and then set the place on fire. In effect, he was primitively "messing up the nest."

Q: How do these kids handle their conflicting feelings and actions?

A: "Splitting" is the mechanism these kids use. They divide themselves and others into good and bad. They have alternate rather than simultaneous feelings. These kids with character disorders are not psychotic. Psychotics use repression, stating, "I love my mother," while dreaming of killing her. The severe character disorders have a conscious awareness and will disavow rather than deny their actions. When you ask them, for example, "You used to love your mother, what happened?", their response is, "Well, that was then. I don't love her now."

Q: How do you treat these types of kids?

A: You remind them gingerly about what they are doing. You get them to imagine these alternating and contradictory patterns. You help them to see how they split in their feelings and actions. Often, these patterns have been learned at home. Their mothers would alternate in their dealings with these boys by lavishing them with kisses and hugs, on the one hand, and abandoning them or assuming they could take care of themselves prematurely, on the other hand.

Q: Is arson the offense that usually brings these troubled kids to treatment?

A: No. It is rarely that they get caught for arson. But one in five or six of the wards that we treat has set fires.

Q: How are the juvenile arsonists treated by the other wards
    in the institution? Because they are passive-aggressives, are
    they more vulnerable to sexual assault from the other
    wards?

A: Some of them are wild and dangerous. Most are vulnerable.
    Sexual assault probably occurs, but it is not clear-cut.

Q: How do you wean them of their dependency on the treat-
    ment program once they are ready to be released from
    prison?

A: Firesetters are not that overtly dependent. They are not the
    most dependent of the wards, unless they are psychotic.
    One black boy, twenty, with a high IQ, had three types of
    medication that he would refuse to take so that he could
    not get better and therefore be released. Eventually, he was
    released, but he would continue to walk nine miles each
    day to the prison gate to call to his therapist. Even when
    he was on the outside, he would refuse to take his medi-
    cine, which would help regulate his [manic-depressive]
    moods. Recently, he was shot through the back and killed
    by a police officer in an attempted bank robbery.

Q: Do you treat the firesetters in any type of group therapy?

A: No. We do not conduct group therapy with just all fireset-
    ters. That might be a good idea. One reason that we have
    not is that we don't have enough firesetters at any one time.
    Also, they are usually too varied in terms of the reasons
    that they turned to fire as an acting-out behavior. We group
    wards according to what therapeutic approach is best suited
    to them rather than what their incarcerating offense was.

Q: Do they suffer from particular sensory deprivation?

A: They lack the capacity for imagery. If they have dreams,
    they are often of a raw, primitive effect rather than content.
    They dream about being mad or scared rather than the dy-
    namics of the dream itself. [In other words, they do not
    remember the content of the dream but instead recollect
    only that they were frightened.] Often, they disavow in
    their dreams, which is indicative of their splitting pattern.
    They disavow because the fantasies that accompany their

dreams are so threatening and frightening. Lying and denying fantasies are difficult to talk about.

Q: Are there any improvements that you would like to see the Youth Authority make with regard to the treatment of firesetters?

A: One could argue for more research into this area of arson. The Youth Authority has had special programs in the past. For a time, it was drug abuse. Now, the mood is to be hard on criminals. I could see a need for an emphasis on special target populations such as firesetters. You could justify it on the basis of protecting the public and for public health reasons. More likely, the continued emphasis will be personality profiles and background-related patterns. The offense that brings these youngsters in here is often least significant.

Chapter Thirteen

STRATEGIES FOR THE FUTURE

One reason why America is burning, according to national government officials, is that Americans not only are indifferent to fire as a national problem but are similarly careless about fire in their personal lives. Though the public is aroused over safety issues regarding consumer products or the environment, fire safety is not one of their chief concerns. Few private homes have fire extinguishers; even fewer have fire detection systems. Too many multiple-family dwellings and establishments have yet to install automatic equipment for putting out fires. And often, when fire does strike, ignorance of proper escape routes leads to panic, which further exacerbates the danger of the fire.[1]

One of the first strategies, therefore, for the future is to work toward greater fire-safety education and public awareness. With the patterns outlined above typifying the behavior of the American public, it is no wonder that young children and juveniles have not been taught proper fire-safety procedures. Without such instruction, youngsters, on their own, play with matches and learn how to torch—as this book shows.

This criticism is not meant to imply that the public is now doing nothing about fire education. On the contrary, several cities have recently developed innovative community- and school-based educational programs. However, in all these programs, financial cutbacks and scarce resources have meant that the programs are not as extensive and effective as they could, and should, be.

In Southern California, many elementary schools continue to offer an educational unit on proper fire safety. Beginning in 1980, the Los Angeles school district inaugurated a "team" educational approach. Usually, four team members—comprised of volunteers from womens' service clubs, other civilian organizations, and members of the fire departments and the forestry service—present half-hour sessions in the lower elementary grades. Often accompanied by someone dressed as "Smokey the Bear," the team members show the youngest children (through the second grade) a fire prevention film, such as *Mr. Flame*; go through Smokey's rules, such as being careful with matches, turning over any matches found to adults, and reporting any fires; and show the class items from a mystery box, such as charred pieces of wood, which the children are asked to identify. When the session is over, each child is made a Junior Forest Ranger and is designated as Smokey's Helper.[2]

In recent years, several fire departments have developed programs in which fire fighters demonstrate their paraphernalia to young children, since, with the popularity of the *Star Wars* films, some children have confused fire fighters with the villain, Darth Vader. These children are instructed to view fire fighters as friends, not threats.

Additional educational programs have been developed for younger and older elementary-school children by other organizations. The Hartford Insurance Company, for example, has developed a school-based Junior Fire Marshall Program. This serves as a kind of social and service club for students who are concerned about fire.

For the slightly older junior-high-school students, other programs have been initiated. One educational program includes a variety of media presentations, along with a so-called room of fire hazards. This "room" consists of fifteen simulated fire hazards, among which are overloaded wall sockets, cigarette butts in chair cushions, and paint and gasoline cans near wall heaters. Students tour this converted classroom, note which hazards they've observed, and compare their responses with those made by a fire safety inspector.

Many local fire departments have developed a junior fire patrol. Two similar programs in Southern California are a Junior Firesetters Program, begun in San Bernardino County by two battalion fire chiefs, and a program aimed at junior-high-school students by the youth-awareness subcommittee of the Mayor of Los Angeles' Arson Suppression Task Force. These programs are aimed at making the youngsters aware of the major financial hardship and life-threatening circumstances caused by arson and fire vandalism. Part of the program includes student visiting to burn wards.

Many of these community-based programs are modeled on the Explorer's scouting program. And like the remarkably successful Firehawk program discussed in Chapter 12, these other programs provide troubled youths—some of whom who have set fires—with proper supervision by fire-safety personnel.

In summary, these varied educational strategies aimed at the young involve the concerted efforts of parents, fire-safety personnel, concerned citizen groups, and educators, as well as elected public officials. The school- and community-based programs have as their common goal the helping of youngsters to gain an understanding of the proper role of fire in our society.

These important fire-safety efforts do not stop with the young. Each year in the second week of October, in recognition of the great Chicago fire of 1871—which sparked a disaster of major proportions, leaving 200 people dead, 100,000 homeless, 17,500 buildings in ruins, and 2,100 acres of the city charred—the nation observes Fire

Prevention Week. Many local communities and fire departments plan events that are designed to increase public awareness about fire and to assist people in becoming better prepared for fire if it strikes.

During Fire Prevention Week, parents are encouraged to take their kids to visit the neighborhood firehouse, and to identify and correct fire hazards in their own homes. Often, local fire departments hold a special "Pump-In Day," featuring a display of antique and classic fire-fighting apparatus and pumping demonstrations. A number of communities across the country have set up special fire fighter's museums, which highlight old equipment and photographs. These facilities are especially recognized during that week.[3]

Fire Prevention Week also marks the occasion for the annual publishing of fire safety "tips" by a nationally syndicated newspaper columnist. Noting that each season has its own special fire hazards, we quote from this important public-service announcement:

> FALL: If you enjoy camping, select a tent made of flame-resistant fabric. Pack a reliable flashlight with plenty of extra batteries to light the inside of your tent—never use matches or candles. When building a campfire, place it downwind of your tent. And NEVER try to hasten the burning by using gasoline or other flammable liquid starters.
>
> If you use your fireplace, have your chimney professionally cleaned in the fall to make sure it's in good condition for the coming season.
>
> WINTER: More fires occur during winter than in any other season. The reasons: home heating and the holiday season.
>
> If you use a portable heater, be sure it is placed away from combustibles—draperies, furniture, paper, etc. Remember, the surface heat of some portable heaters may reach 500 degrees, so keep a careful watch on your children

and warn them to keep away from heaters. Hospitals are treating an increasing number of patients with burns resulting from contact with the outside surface of some portable heaters.

For a merry Christmas, choose a Christmas tree that does not have shedding needles, and keep it standing in water while it is in the house. If you choose an artificial tree, choose one that is flame-resistant.

After holiday parties, before retiring, check your ashtrays for smoldering cigarette butts, and carefully examine all upholstered chairs and sofas to make sure that no "live" cigarette butts have fallen between the cushions. Remember, most house fires occur between 8 P.M. and 8 A.M., when people are sleeping.

SPRING: Take spring cleaning seriously—clean out your attic, basement, garage and workshop. Throw out trash, especially combustibles like rags, newspapers, magazines, boxes and scraps of wood. Never smoke while fueling gas-powered lawn mowers or chain saws. If you must store gasoline, store it in a ventilated area in a can designed especially for that purpose. And store oil rags and paint in a cool place in tightly sealed metal containers.

SUMMER: When cooking out, NEVER use flammable liquids near live coals. An explosion or flash fire could result. When you're finished with cooking, soak the coals with water and make absolutely sure they're out when you leave. Smoldering coals that appear to be "dead" can reignite as much as a day later! If you use a propane gas grill, always have the lighted match in position BEFORE turning on the gas.

Some tips for all seasons:

Never smoke in bed.

Never leave invalids or small children alone in the house—not even for a "few minutes."

Never use flammable liquids for dry-cleaning indoors.

Have periodic fire drills in your home to be sure everyone knows what to do in case of fire.

Keep easy-to-use fire extinguishers in your kitchen, cottage, back bedrooms and on your boat. And if you can afford smoke detectors, install them and be sure they are always dust-free and in working order.

The phone number of your Fire Department should be taped to every telephone in your house. If it isn't, should a fire occur, don't waste time trying to find it; get out, and call from a neighbor's house. And once you are out, stay out. No treasure is worth risking your life for.[4]

These fire-safety "tips" are important and should be followed. But as our book shows, the fire problem may go beyond the lack of good fire-safety education.

A second strategy for the future involves the extension and coordination of services aimed at assisting the child who has a propensity for setting fires. As we have noted throughout this book, firesetting children seem to be less able than other children to vent their anger or frustration in socially approved ways. Usually, their firesetting episode is the result of a triggering event or circumstances resulting in sad, lonely feelings that turn into angry feelings and culminate in the use of matches or a lighter to set something afire.

These troubled youngsters must be assisted in identifying the reasons behind their "urge to burn" and must be provided with alternative ways, other than fire, to deal with this urge. Being made aware that a certain feeling triggers a fire response that gets them into trouble, these youngsters—from young to old and from least to most severe—can be counseled to develop productive ways to vent their anger and to resolve their feelings of helplessness.

As our book demonstrates, behavioral characteristics, the types of fires set, the fires set by different age groups, psychological profiles, and other social patterns that we have delineated—all provide an abundance of clues that will serve to identify the child at risk. What is now needed is the development of greater coordination between those who observe the child on a daily basis—such as parents, siblings, other relatives, schoolteachers, school counselors, neighbors, other children, fire personnel, clergy, and the general public—with the appropriate officials, who can provide the proper counseling and intervention. The mere examination of the behavioral problems checklist, for instance, can give parents, teachers, and school counselors invaluable information about and insight into the seriousness of a child's problems. As we have shown, potential and current firesetters can be identified. Their behavior serves as a "red flag," calling attention to their problem state.

A third key strategy for the future with regard to curbing juvenile arson, therefore, is the coordination of efforts on the part of public officials who are concerned about these firesetters. Why, for instance, could not a nationally based service be put in operation by a National Fire Safety Council, under the direction of the U.S. Fire Administration, to provide concerned parents with a toll-free "hotline" service. By dialing this number, parents could get information about the variety of services that are available in their local area. This coordinated service would require that all services be identified, categorized, and advertised. As it stands now, many of these services are in operation, but there is duplication, lack of knowledge about their availability, and fear of severe punitive measures, and the public is not often aware of how to contact them. Of urgent need, therefore, is a Firesetters Intervention Service of sorts, to coordinate, articulate, and publicize the programs that are available.

Another possible program would be an Arsonists Anonymous program, modeled after the Alcoholics Anonymous and Weight Watchers organizations, which provide

services for reformed (and reforming) drinkers and over-
eaters. Such a support group, aimed at the person prone
to setting fires, could help some older teenage and adult
firesetters to deal more effectively with those moods and
feelings that accompany their "cravings" for fire. Often,
a support group of individuals who share a behavioral
problem can do wonders in discouraging the continuation
of that behavior. There is no reason to think that such a
program cannot also benefit certain arsonists. To our
knowledge, no such program is in operation (except for
certain group-therapy programs within the prison or hospital setting).

One observer has viewed firesetting behavior as a
threefold process: an interaction between historical factors
that predispose a person to a variety of antisocial acts; environmental and social patterns that teach an individual
to play with fire; and immediate conditions that motivate
the firesetting act.[5] In other words, as we stated in the
opening chapter, we *do* know those factors that set the
firesetting process in operation. And because we know,
we should be able to do something both to intervene in
and to correct the incendiary activity.

Firesetting among white, middle-class youth is on the
rise. As our study has shown, areas across the nation, like
San Bernardino County, are attempting to cope with this
"epidemic of arson." Conservatives and liberals alike have
voiced concern.

Overwhelmingly, firesetters come from troubled families. Whether the exact nature of their respective problems
is due to family instability, problem parent–child interaction, absent fathers, parental pathology, or overindul-
gent and inconsistent mothers, the fact is clear that these
juveniles are at risk because of family disturbances.

Further, as our behavioral characteristics' indicators
have demonstrated, firesetting is not the only problem

area that these youngsters share. Firesetters, compared to nonfiresetters, exhibit such problems as stealing, truancy, excessive fantasizing, aggression, destructiveness, hyperactivity, sleep disturbances, a lack of impulse control, running away from home, and a generalized behavior disturbance. Likewise, these youngsters have difficulties in school and with peers. Some even have constitutional difficulties, including physical abnormalities. Others have histories of enuresis and sexual dysfunctioning.

Given that these disturbed children from troubled families manifest a variety of maladaptive behaviors, it is important to note what makes them turn to firesetting as an expression of their frustration, anger, or revenge. Having learned at an early age that playing with fire satisfies a certain need, these youngsters continue a pattern in which firesetting becomes the means by which stress is reduced. The chain of response, as we have stated, must be broken.

With younger firesetters, stress events such as a divorce, a death in the family, or the arrival of a new stepparent or sibling often precede the firesetting episode. With teenagers, the act is often tied to antagonism toward school and parental authority or to peer pressure and peer acceptance or is a result of incest and sexual abuse. Other youngsters are merely excited by the act of setting fires and the attention given to the fires by the fire fighters, the public, and the press. For some, the act is fashioned from a need for revenge and is an expression of rage and anger. And for some with psychotic disorders, the incendiary act is tied to a hallucinatory command.

As we have observed, effective treatment of firesetting, like the treatment of other forms of socially maladaptive behavior, requires early detection and appropriate intervention. Procedures such as those generated by the classification manual, as well as programs in fire safety such as those begun by the San Bernardino County Probation Department—and similar programs nationwide—are to be commended for providing the services of intervention to the general public. In the hands of fire-safety personnel, these programs have helped to clarify the strategies for intervention and treatment—whether they be in the chaotic family milieu, in the area of fire play, or in the area of stimulus or reinforcement control.

We hope that—with the continued and expanding efforts of fire departments, probation departments, and other social service agencies across the country in these areas of juvenile fire prevention, intervention, and treatment—a nationwide response is emerging to successfully combat and counsel America's troubled youth—these kids who torch.

NOTES

Chapter 1

1. Newspaper accounts of actual fire incidents are interspersed throughout this book in edited form. In all instances, identifying characteristics, such as names and locations, have been altered. The exact citation, however, is given. *Los Angeles Times* (10 October 1983), Part II, p. 6.
2. *Uniform Crime Report for the United States* (Washington, D.C.: U.S. Department of Justice, Federal Bureau of Investigation, 1982).
3. Ibid.

Chapter 2

1. Marc Leepson, "Arsonists at Work," *Sacramento Bee* (23 December 1982) p. B-10.
2. Ibid., p. B-1.
3. *Uniform Crime Report for the United States* (Washington, D.C.: U.S. Department of Justice, Federal Bureau of Investigation, 1982).
4. D. D. Carr *et al.* "Arson and Aetna," Aetna Life & Casualty (March 1979).
5. Ibid.
6. *Arson Prevention and Control* (Washington, D.C.: U.S. Department of Justice, January 1980).
7. Kenneth Fineman, Charles S. Brudo, Esther S. Brudo, *et al.*, *Interviewing and Counseling Juvenile Firesetters* (Washington, D.C.: United States Fire Administration, November 1979).
8. John M. MacDonald, *Bombers and Firesetters* (Springfield, Ill.: Charles C Thomas, 1977), p. 179.
9. Ibid., p. 180.
10. Ibid.
11. Ibid., p. 182.
12. Ibid.

13. N. D. C. Lewis and H. Yarnell, "Pathological Firesetting (Pyro-mania)," *Nervous and Mental Disease Monographs*, No. 82 (1951).
14. Ibid.
15. Ibid.
16. Kenneth R. Fineman, "Firesetting in Childhood and Adolescence," *Psychiatric Clinics of North America*, 3 (December 1980), pp. 483–500.
17. G. A. Heath, W. F. Gayton, and V. A. Hardesty, "Childhood Firesetting," *Canadian Psychiatric Association Journal* 21 (1976), 229–237.
18. American Psychiatric Association, *Diagnostic and Statistical Manual of Mental Disorders*, 3rd ed. (Washington, D.C.: American Psychiatric Association, 1980).
19. *Uniform Crime Report*, 1982.

Chapter 3

1. N. D. C. Lewis and H. Yarnell, "Pathological Firesetting (Pyro-mania)," *Nervous and Mental Disease Monographs*, No. 82 (1951).
2. R. G. Vreeland and M. B. Waller, *The Psychology of Firesetting: A Review and Appraisal* (Washington, D.C.: U.S. Department of Commerce, National Bureau of Standards, 1979).
3. Kenneth Fineman, Charles S. Brudo, Esther S. Brudo, *et al.*, *Interviewing and Counseling Juvenile Firesetters* (Washington, D.C.: United States Fire Administration, November 1979).
4. Subsequent chapters incorporate the case files of these youngsters and an additional thirty-four juvenile arsonists who were also apprehended in this same time period in San Bernardino County, but whose case files remain incomplete.
5. William S. Folkman, *Children-Caused Fires—How to Prevent Them* (Sacramento, CA: California Pacific Southwest Forest and Range Experiment Station, 1972).
6. W. S. Folkman and E. Y. Siegelman, *Youthful Firesetters: An Exploratory Study in Personality and Background* (Washington, D.C.: U.S. Department of Agriculture, Forest Service, 1971).
7. For example, one of our findings shows that younger firesetters are more apt to be cruel to animals than older firesetters. One could argue convincingly that older firesetters do not torture their own pets in front of their parents; they are more likely to find some poor, stray animal on the street—out of their parents' sight. Moreover, because firesetters frequently come from broken homes, where it is more likely that the parent of an older child (with no

spouse around) is out working during the day, it is probable that
the parent does not always know what her or his offspring is doing.

8. I. Kaufman, L. W. Heims, and D. E. Reiser, "A Reevaluation of
the Psychodynamics of Firesetting," *American Journal of Orthopsychiatry* 31 (1961), 123–137.
9. Lewis and Yarnell.
10. B. Nurcombe, "Children Who Set Fires," *Medical Journal of Australia*
(April 1964), 577–584.
11. E. Siegelman, *Children Who Set Fires: An Exploratory Study*. Conducted for the Resources Agency of California, Department of Con-
servation, Division of Forestry, 1969.
12. Melvin L. Kohn, *Class and Conformity* (Washington, D.C.: Dorsey
Press, 1969).
13. H. Yarnell, "Firesetting in Children," *American Journal of Orthopsychiatry* 10 (1940), 262–286.
14. Kaufman, Heims, and Reiser.
15. D. Kafry, *Fire Survival Skills: Who Plays with Matches?* Technical report for Pacific Southwest Forest and Range Experiment Stations,
U.S. Department of Agriculture, Washington, D.C., 1978.
16. T. A. Vandersall and J. M. Weiner, "Children Who Set Fires," *Archives of General Psychiatry* 22 (1970), 63–71.
17. Nurcombe.
18. Ibid.
19. G. R. Patterson, "The Aggressive Child: Victim and Architect of a
Coercive System," in L. A. Mamerlynck, L. C. Handy, and E. J.
Marsh (eds.), *Behavioral Modification and Families* (New York: Brun-
ner/Mazel, 1976).
20. E. Y. Siegelman and W. S. Folkman, *Youthful Firesetters: An Exploratory Study in Personality and Background* (Springfield, Va.: U.S.
Department of Agriculture, Forest Service, 1971).
21. D. S. Hellman and N. Blackman, "Enuresis, Firesetting, and Cruelty to Animals: A Triad Predictive of Adult Crime," *American Journal of Psychiatry* 122 (1966), 1431–1435.

Chapter 4

1. "4 Sisters Badly Burned Playing With Matches," *Los Angeles Times*
(9 April 1983), Part II, p. 1.
2. Helen G. Smith, "Mom, Son Injured: 2 Children Killed in Norwalk
Blaze," *Long Beach Independent Press Telegram* (4 April 1983), p. A-
3.

3. San Bernardino County, *Criminal Justice Profile, 1981,* State of California, Bureau of Criminal Statistics, Sacramento, California.
4. Ibid.
5. D. Kafry, *Fire Survival Skills: Who Plays with Matches?* Technical report for Pacific Southwest Forest and Range Experiment Stations, U.S. Department of Agriculture, 1978.
6. Ibid.
7. T. A. Vandersall and J. M. Weiner, "Children Who Set Fires," *Archives of General Psychiatry* 22 (1970), 63–71.
8. B. Nurcombe, "Children Who Set Fires," *Medical Journal of Australia* (April 1964), 577–584.

Chapter 5

1. "Stockton Boy, 3, Reportedly Sets Twin Sisters Afire," *Los Angeles Times* (10 February 1983), Part II, p. 2.
2. Kenneth R. Fineman, in a presentation to the California Conference of Arson Investigators, El Monte, California, 15 December 1983.
3. I. Kaufman, L. W. Heims, and D. E. Reiser, "A Reevaluation of the Psychodynamics of Firesetting," *American Journal of Orthopsychiatry*, 31 (1961), 123–137.
4. M. M. Miller, "A Group Therapeutic Approach to a Case of Bedwetting and Fire Setting with the Aid of Hypnoanalysis," *Group Psychotherapy* 10 (1957), 181–190.
5. O. Fenichel, *The Psychoanalytic Theory of Neurosis* (New York: Norton, 1945), pp. 371–372.

Chapter 6

1. Joy Horowitz, "Firesetting Youths—Why They Do It," *Los Angeles Times* (18 September 1979), Section V, p. 1.
2. "Gains Made in War on Arson?" *Los Angeles Times* (28 October 1979), B, p. 1.
3. "Mexican National Booked in LA Fire That Killed 24," *Sacramento Bee* (24 December 1982), Section A, p. 5.
4. Tina May, "Arsonists Aren't Wild-Eyed Crooks," *The Sun* (23 September 1979), Section B, p. 1.
5. Ibid.
6. "Arson: How to Defend against the Most Destructive School Crime," *School Security* 1 (December 1976), 1–8.
7. Ibid.

8. W. J. Moretz, "Psychology's Understanding of Arson: What Do We Know, and What Do We Need to Know?" *Fire and Arson Investigator* 28(1) (1977), 45–52.
9. San Bernardino County, Criminal Justice Profile, 1981, State of California, Bureau of Criminal Statistics, Sacramento, California.
10. Horowitz, p. 1.
11. John S. Barracato, *Fire . . . Is It Arson?* Aetna Life & Casualty, 1979, pp. 3–10.

Chapter 7

1. Joy Horowitz, "Firesetting Youths—Why They Do It," *Los Angeles Times* (18 September 1979), Part V, p. 1.
2. Roland J. Chilton and Gerald E. Markle, "Family Disruption, Delinquent Conduct and the Effect of Subclassification," *American Sociological Review* 37 (February 1972), 93–99.
3. Sheldon Glueck and Eleanor Glueck, *Unraveling Juvenile Delinquency* (Cambridge: Harvard University Press, 1950), pp. 88–89.
4. Ruth S. Cavan and Theodore N. Ferdinand, *Juvenile Delinquency* (New York: Harper & Row, 1981).
5. Glueck and Glueck.
6. Stanton E. Samenow, *Inside the Criminal Mind* (New York: Times Books, 1984).
7. Stanton E. Samenow, "Is It Always the Parents' Fault?" *Family Weekly* (15 January 1984), p. 6.

Chapter 8

1. This is more of a composite clipping than one based on an actual incident. Sections are modified from an article titled "Young Killer's Stepdad Faces Sex Investigation," *Fresno Bee* (30 December 1983), Part C, p. 11.
2. Judith M. Bardwick, *Psychology of Women* (New York: Harper & Row, 1971).
3. H. Yarnell, "Firesetting in Children," *American Journal of Orthopsychiatry* 10 (1940), 262–286.
4. N. D. C. Lewis and H. Yarnell, "Pathological Firesetting (Pyromania)," *Nervous and Mental Disease Monographs*, No. 82 (1951).
5. Ibid.
6. Ibid.
7. Ruth S. Cavan and Theodore N. Ferdinand, *Juvenile Delinquency* (New York: Harper and Row), p. 244.

8. Nicholas A. Groth, with H. Jean Bernbaum, *Men Who Rape: The Psychology of the Offender* (New York: Plenum Press, 1979).
9. Suzanne M. Sgroi, *Handbook of Clinical Intervention in Child Sexual Abuse* (Boston, Mass.: D. C. Heath, 1982).
10. T. G. Tennet, A. McQuaid, T. Louhnane, *et al.*, "Female Arsonists," *British Journal of Psychiatry* 119 (1971), 497–502.
11. J. J. Michaels, *Disorders of Character* (Springfield, Ill.: Charles C Thomas, 1955).
12. Brendan P. Battle and Paul B. Weston, *Arson* (New York: Greenberg Publishers, 1954).
13. Lewis and Yarnell.
14. Battle and Weston.
15. Joseph Harry, *Gay Children Grown Up* (New York: Praeger, 1982).

Chapter 9

1. Anthony O. Rider, "The Firesetter: A Psychological Profile," in *Arson* (Washington, D.C.: Resource Exchange Bulletin, U.S. Fire Administration, October 1980), pp. 22–29.
2. Joy Horowitz, "Firesetting Youths—Why They Do It," *Los Angeles Times* (18 September 1979), Section V, p. 1.
3. Dave Larsen, "Youths and Arson Equal a Combustible Combination," *Los Angeles Times* (21 September 1980), Part X, p. 1.
4. Susan Ager, "Kids Who Kill," *The Register* (5 May 1983), Section D, p. 1.
5. L. B. Macht and J. E. Mack, "The Firesetter Syndrome," *Psychiatry* 31 (1968), 277–288.
6. M. Schmidelberg, "Pathological Firesetters," *Journal of Criminal Law, Criminology and Police Science* 44 (1953), 30–39.
7. D. S. Hellman and N. Blackman, "Enuresis, Firesetting, and Cruelty to Animals: A Triad Predictive of Adult Crime," *American Journal of Psychiatry* 122 (1966), 1431–1435.
8. Developed by Marguerite Q. Warren, who worked with delinquents in a state community treatment project in California in the 1960s.
9. Ruth S. Cavan and Theodore N. Ferdinand, *Juvenile Delinquency* (New York: Harper & Row, 1981).
10. D. J. Barlett, W. P. Hurley, C. R. Brand, *et al.*, "Chromosomes of Male Patients in a Security Hospital," *Nature* 219 (1968), 351–354.
11. Wayne S. Wooden and Jay Parker, *Men behind Bars: Sexual Exploitation in Prison* (New York: Plenum Press, 1982).

Chapter 10

1. *Los Angeles Times* (7 October 1983), p. 2.
2. N. D. C. Lewis and H. Yarnell, "Pathological Firesetting (Pyromania)," *Nervous and Mental Disease Monographs*, No. 82 (1951).
3. John D. DeHaan, *Kirk's Fire Investigation* (New York: Wiley, 1983).

Chapter 11

1. "Owner of House Held in Blast and Fire That Killed Two Men," *Independent Press Telegram* (8 August 1983), p. 3.
2. "State Offers $5,000 Reward in Arson Blaze," *Los Angeles Times* (8 August 1983), p. 7.
3. "The Arson File," *Los Angeles Magazine* (August 1982), p. 178.
4. James Gardner *et al.*, *Arson Prevention and Control* (Washington, D.C.: U.S. Department of Justice, January 1980).
5. John F. Bourdreau *et al.*, *Arson and Arson Investigation* (Washington, D.C.: National Institute of Law Enforcement and Criminal Justice, U.S. Department of Justice, October 1977).
6. Ibid.
7. Ibid.
8. John D. DeHaan, *Kirk's Fire Investigation* (New York: Wiley, 1983).
9. Ibid.
10. D. J. Icove and H. R. Crisman, "Application of Pattern Recognition in Arson Investigation," *Fire Technology* 11 (February 1975), 35–41.
11. Bourdreau *et al.*
12. Robert Studer, "Witness Is Best Tool against Arson," *Sacramento Union* (5 November 1978), p. 3.
13. Ibid.
14. *We TIP*, pamphlet available from P.O. Box 740, Ontario, CA 91761.

Chapter 12

1. For additional information, contact CPC Cedar Hills Hospital in Portland, Oregon, for a brochure describing their treatment protocol developed by J. Douglas Myers, Ph.D., and the staff of Cedar Hills Hospital.
2. David Holmstrom, "Firemen's Companionship Keeps Boys from Becoming Fire-Setters," *The Christian Science Monitor* (2 November 1983), p. 7.

3. Carl F. Jesness, "Comparative Effectiveness of Two Institutional Treatment Programs for Delinquents," *Child Care Quarterly* (Winter 1971–1972), 120–130.
4. Rudy A. Haapanen and Carl F. Jesness, *Early Identification of the Chronic Offender* (Sacramento: State of California Department of the Youth Authority, February 1982).

Chapter 13

1. Richard Bland *et al.*, *America Burning, The Report of the National Commission on Fire Prevention and Control* (Washington, D.C.: U.S. Government Printing Office, 1973).
2. "Youth and Arson Equal a Combustible Combination," *Los Angeles Times* (21 September 1980), Part X, p. 1.
3. "Fire Prevention Week Begins Sunday," *Long Beach Independent Press Telegram* (8 October 1983), p. A-7.
4. Abigail Van Buren, "Fire Safety Never Goes Out of Season," *Los Angeles Times* (10 October 1983), Part II, p. 6. Copyright 1983 by Universal Press Syndicate. Reprinted by permission.
5. Kenneth R. Fineman, "Firesetting in Childhood and Adolescence," *Psychiatric Clinics of North America* 3 (December 1980), pp. 483–500.

Appendix A

QUESTIONNAIRES

QUESTIONNAIRE 1
FAMILY INTERVIEW AND EVALUATION FORM
("QUESTIONS TO BE ASKED OF PARENTS")

Interviewer _____ Date _____

Juvenile's name _____ Sex __ DOB _____

Ethnicity/race _____

Address _____ Phone _____

School attended _____ Grade _____

Address _____

Mother's name _____

Father's name _____

Marital status: __ Married __ Single __ Divorced
__ Widowed/Separated

Number of children in family __ Birth order of juvenile __

1. Is child on medication? __ yes __ no What type? __

   _____

2. Has child been regarded as hyperkinetic or as having a
   neurological dysfunction?

   _____

3. Is this your own child? __ yes __ foster __ adopted

4. Has there been a recent change in family structure?
   __ divorce __ new baby __ death of relative __ other

5. Has the child been under severe stress in the past six

Questionnaire 1 and the "Parent Questionnaire" of Questionnaire 2 are re-
produced from *Interviewing and Counseling Juvenile Firesetters* by the Federal Emergency Management Agency, U.S. Fire Administration—National
Fire Academy (Washington, D.C.: U.S. Government Printing Office, 1980).

215

months? (i.e., moved to another neighborhood or school, or lost friends)
Explain _____
_____

6. Does the child have a physical ailment? (Explain) ___
7. Is the child physically immature for age? __ yes __ no
8. How do you normally discipline the child? __ spank __ isolate __ withdraw privileges __ yell __ other (Explain) _____
_____

9. How often is the discipline given? _____
10. Was this his/her first fire? _____
How many others set? _____
11. What was set on fire? __ paper, trash, or leaves __ child's own property __ child's room __ self, animals, people __ other person's property __ other
Explain _____
_____

12. Materials used to start fire __ matches __ lighter __ other
Explain _____
13. How did child get material to start fire? __ found it __ went out of his/her way to acquire it __ other
Explain _____
14. Is the child's curiosity about fire __ mild __ moderate __ extreme
15. Was child pressured or coerced into firesetting behavior by peers? __ yes __ no
16. Was the fire in question an accident? __ yes __ no
17. Was the child attempting to do harm or to destroy property by setting the fire? __ yes __ no
18. Was the fire set because the child was incapable of understanding what he/she was doing? __ yes __ no
19. Was the child properly supervised during the firesetting incident? __ yes __ no
20. Does the child know the proper use of matches and/or fire? __ yes __ no

21. Did the child panic when the fire got out of control?
 __ yes __ no
22. Did the child attempt to get help? __ yes __ no
23. Was anyone with the child when the fire was set? __ yes
 __ no
 If yes, who _____
 (Address)   (Phone)

 _____
 _____
 _____

Additional Observations Regarding Child's Home and Parents:

(Don't ask parents *all* the following questions. Most questions are based on information or observations.)

24. Was outside of residence sloppy? __ yes __ no
25. Was inside of residence sloppy? __ yes __ no
26. Does parent(s) appear indifferent toward child?
 __ Mother __ Father
27. Does parent(s) appear hostile toward child?
 __ Mother __ Father
28. Does child appear neglected? __ yes __ no
29. Does child appear abused? __ yes __ no
30. Is there an indication that fire was precipitated by family difficulties or family arguments? __ yes __ no
31. Is there an indication that the fire was started after the child became angry at another person or himself/herself?
 __ yes __ no
32. Is there an indication that the fire was set primarily to destroy something or someone? __ yes __ no
33. Is there an indication that the fire was set primarily because the child was told that he/she could not play with fire? __ yes __ no
34. Is there an indication that the child perceives magical qualities to fire? __ yes __ no

35. Does the child deny interest in fire if information to the contrary is available? __ yes __ no
36. Does the fire appear to be a "cry for help" from the child? __ yes __ no
37. Does it appear that parenting has been inadequate or infrequent for this child? __ yes __ no
38. Does the fire appear to be positive or funny to the child? __ yes __ no
39. Does the fire appear to bolster the child's feelings of power or self-confidence? __ yes __ no
40. Does __ mother __ father appear indifferent to or unconcerned about the present situation?
41. Does __ mother __ father appear to be of subnormal intelligence?
42. Does __ mother __ father appear to be in poor contact with reality?
43. Does __ mother __ father appear to be inappropriately angry or moody?

PARENT QUESTIONNAIRE

PARENT(s): Please fill out this form *as soon as possible*. Make a check mark under the answer—"never," "sometimes," or "frequently"—that best describes your child for every question. Ask any questions you have. We want to know if the child exhibits the following behavior. When marking the form consider all parts of the child's life (at home, at school, etc.) where these behaviors might be present.

Behavior	Never	Sometimes	Frequently
Hyperactivity			
Lack of concentration			
Learning problems (home or school)			
Behavior problems in school			

Behavior	Never	Sometimes	Frequently
Impulsive (acts before thinking)			
Impatient			
Accidents			
Convulsions or "spells"			
Wets during day			
Extreme mood swings			
Need for security			
Need for affection			
Depression			
Unusual movements—tics			
Stuttering			
Bedwetting (after age three)			
Soiling (after age three)			
Lying			
Excessive and uncontrolled anger			
Violence			
Stealing			
Truancy			
Cruelty to animals			
Cruelty to children			
Fighting with peers			
Fighting with siblings			
Destroys toys of others			
Destroys own toys			
Runs away from home or school			
Disobeys			
Long history of severe behavioral difficulties			
Child is a poor loser			

Behavior	Never	Sometimes	Frequently
Child expresses anger by hurting other's things			
Child expresses anger by hurting self or something she/he likes			
Child has been in trouble with the police			
Easily led by peers			
Jealousy			
Temper tantrums			
Doesn't play with other children			
Shows off			
Severe depressions or withdrawal			
Child is good in sports			
Shyness			
Extreme goodness			
Sexual activity with others			
Stomachaches			
Nightmares			
Other sleep or waking problems			
Anxiety			
Fantasizing			
Poor or no eye contact			
Child has twitches (eyes, face, etc.)			
Crying			
Nail biting			
Vomiting			
Thumb sucking			
Aches and pains			
Chewing odd things			

Behavior	Never	Sometimes	Frequently
Constipation			
Diarrhea			
Masturbation			
Curiosity about fire			
Plays with fire			
Panicked when fire got out of control			
Fires set some distance from child's home			
Child proud or boastful regarding firesetting			
Stares at fires for long periods of time			
Daydreams or talks about fire			
Unusual look on child's face as he/she frequently stares at fires			
Family discord			
Father or mother absent			
Family has moved with child			
Child has seen a therapist			
Other family member has seen a therapist			
Parent has serious health problem			
Marriage is unhappy			
Mother's discipline is effective			
Father's discipline is effective			
Unusual fantasies			
Strange thought patterns			

Behavior	Never	Sometimes	Frequently
Speech bizarre, illogical, or irrational			
Out of touch with reality			
Strange quality about child			
Self-imposed diets			
Sleepwalking			
Phobias			
Fears			
Child plays alone			

CHILD INTERVIEW FORM
FOR CHILDREN UNDER SEVEN YEARS OF AGE

In order to establish rapport with the child ask as many of the following questions as necessary.

1. What is your name? _____
   Your age? __ What grade are you in? __
2. What do you think of your school? _____
   What do you think of your teachers? _____
3. What do you do for fun, do you have hobbies? _____
4. Do you have a favorite TV program? __ What is it? __
   Who is your favorite person in that show? _____
   Why do you like him/her? _____
5. What does he/she do that makes the show good? ____
6. What food do you like to eat best? _____

When rapport is established, determine level of understanding.
a. using information gained from rapport session above
b. using puppets
c. using toys
d. using games

If you are satisfied that the child has adequate understanding, proceed with the interview.

7. Who is your friend? _____
   What is he/she like? _____
8. What is your favorite thing to do when you play with your friend? _____
   _____
   _____

9. Does your friend set fires? _____
10. How many fires have you set? __ Tell me the different things you have set on fire _____
    One __ More than one __
    __ paper __ child's own property __ other person's property
    __ trash
    __ leaves __ self, animals, other people __ other (explain)
    __ child's room
11. How did you start the fire? _____
    _____
12. Where did you find the ? _____ to start the fire?
    _____
    __ found it __ went out of way to acquire it (explain above)
    __ from another child
13. Who was with you when you started the fire? _____
    Name _____
14. What do you think made you want to start the fire? __
    _____
    __ don't know __ another child told __ to see it burn
    __ to hurt someone __ to destroy something (explain above)
15. Was the fire set after any of the following? __ family fight
    __ being angry at brother or sister __ being angry at a friend

16. Did the fire or fires you have started make you happy or make you laugh?
    __ yes
17. Do you dream about fires at night?   __ yes
18. Do you think about fires in the day?   __ yes
19. Can fire do magical things?   __ yes

To determine the child's mood, need for affection and security, and coherency of thought pattern, ask the following questions with regard to family stability and peer interaction:

20. Do you see your mother a lot, or is she gone a lot?   __ Gone
21. Do you see your father a lot, or is he gone a lot?   __ Gone
22. Tell me about your parents, what are they like?   _____
    _____
23. Tell me about your brothers or sisters, what are they like?

    _____
24. What do you do together with your family?   _____
25. Do you fight a lot with your brothers or sisters?   _____
26. Do you fight a lot with your mother?   _____
27. Do you fight a lot with your father?   _____
28. Do your parents fight a lot with each other?   _____
29. How do your parents punish you when you do something wrong?   _____
    What do they usually punish you for?   _____
    Do you feel they punish you more than they should?   __
30. Has anything bad happened at your house lately?   ____

Rate child as follows:

31. Are child's behavior and mannerisms:
    __ normal __ troubled __ very troubled
32. Is the child's mood:
    __ normal __ troubled __ very troubled
33. Is the child's way of thinking:
    __ normal __ troubled __ very troubled

QUESTIONNAIRE 2

JUVENILE BEHAVIOR STUDY

You have been selected to participate in a study that looks at parents' perceptions of their children's behavior. The responses you give will remain anonymous. You should therefore *not* write your name on this form. An enclosed self-addressed envelope, which requires no postage, is provided so that you may mail in the completed questionnaire. We thank you for your interest and participation.

We ask that you fill out the background information requested below and complete the parent questionnaire that is attached. When completing the form, you should keep in mind the fact that you are answering the questions for only *one* specific child even though you may have more than one. The child whose behavior you will be discussing should fall within the age range of six to sixteen. To assist in narrowing your focus to just one child (of your choice), please answer the following questions.

The youngster that I will be discussing
1. is __ years old.
2. is a ____ (boy or girl).
3. is of _____ racial background.
4. is in the __ grade in school.
5. is my own child __ yes __ foster __ adopted

Other important questions
6. My marital status __ married __ single __ divorced __ widowed/separated
7. I am the child's _____ (mother, father, guardian).
8. Number of children in family __
9. Any recent change in family structure? __ divorce __ new baby __ death of relative __ other (explain)

10. Has the child been under severe stress in the past six months?
    __ no __ yes (explain) _____
11. Does the child have a physical ailment? __ no __ yes (explain) _____
12. Is the child physically immature for age? __ yes __ no
13. How do you normally discipline the child? __ spank __ isolate __ withdraw privileges __ yell __ other (explain) _____
14. Has this child ever got into any trouble with authorities (e.g., teachers, police)? __ no __ yes (explain) __
    _____
15. Has this child ever set any problem fires? __ no __ yes (explain) _____
16. My family's status is __ lower class __ working class __ middle class __ professional class __ upper class
17. My level of education is _____.
18. My occupation is _____.
    Spouse's occupation is _____.

Parent Questionnaire

Please fill out this form by making a check mark under the answer—"never," "sometimes," or "frequently"—that best describes your child for every question. We want to know if the child exhibits the following behavior. When marking the form, consider all parts of the child's life (at home, at school, etc.) where these behaviors might be present.

Behavior	Never	Sometimes	Frequently
Hyperactivity			
Lack of concentration			
Learning problems (home or school)			

Behavior	Never	Sometimes	Frequently
Behavior problems in school			
Impulsive (acts before he/ she thinks)			
Impatient			
Accidents			
Convulsions or "spells"			
Wets during day			
Extreme mood swings			
Need for security			
Need for affection			
Depression			
Unusual movements—tics			
Stuttering			
Bedwetting (after age three)			
Soiling (after age three)			
Lying			
Excessive and uncontrolled anger			
Violence			
Stealing			
Truancy			
Cruelty to animals			
Cruelty to children			
Fighting with peers			
Fighting with siblings			
Destroys toys of others			
Destroys own toys			
Runs away from home or school			
Disobeys			
Long history of severe behavioral difficulties			

Behavior	Never	Sometimes	Frequently
Child is a poor loser			
Child expresses anger by hurting other's things			
Child expresses anger by hurting self or something she/he likes			
Child has been in trouble with the police			
Easily led by peers			
Jealousy			
Temper tantrums			
Doesn't play with other children			
Shows off			
Severe depressions or withdrawal			
Child is good in sports			
Shyness			
Extreme goodness			
Sexual activity with others			
Stomachaches			
Nightmares			
Other sleep or waking problems			
Anxiety			
Fantasizing			
Poor or no eye contact			
Child has twitches (eyes, face, etc.)			
Crying			
Nail biting			
Vomiting			
Thumb sucking			
Aches and pains			
Chewing odd things			

Behavior	Never	Sometimes	Frequently
Constipation			
Diarrhea			
Masturbation			
Curiosity about fire			
Plays with fire			
Panicked when fire got out of control			
Fires set some distance from child's home			
Child proud or boastful regarding firesetting			
Stares at fires for long periods of time			
Daydreams or talks about fire			
Unusual look on child's face as he/she frequently stares at fires			
Family discord			
Father or mother absent			
Family has moved with child			
Child has seen a therapist			
Other family member has seen a therapist			
Parent has serious health problem			
Marriage is unhappy			
Mother's discipline is effective			
Father's discipline is effective			
Unusual fantasies			
Strange thought patterns			

Behavior	Never	Sometimes	Frequently
Speech bizarre, illogical, or irrational			
Out of touch with reality			
Strange quality about child			
Self-imposed diets			
Sleepwalking			
Phobias			
Fears			
Child plays alone			

QUESTIONNAIRE 3

FIRE FIGHTERS STUDY

The following questionnaire has been developed as part of a research program with California State Polytechnic University, Pomona, to determine attitudes that are most consistently found in fire fighters. Please answer all the questions with what you believe to be your most honest feeling, belief, or opinion. You will *not* be asked to provide your name, and the individual responses will be treated with confidentiality.

PART I   BACKGROUND INFORMATION

1. *Sex*
   a. Male
   b. Female
2. *Race/Ethnic Background*
   a. Caucasian
   b. Black
   c. Hispanic
3. *Age*
   a. 18–22
   b. 23–29
   c. 30–40
   d. 41–50
   e. 51 plus
4. *Years of Service*
   a. 0–5
   b. 6–10
   c. 11–15
   d. 16–20
   e. 21 plus
5. *Years in This Department*
   a. 0–5
   b. 6–10
   c. 11–15
   d. 16–20
   e. 21 plus
6. *Level of Education*
   a. High-school graduate
   b. Some college, but no degree
   c. Two-year college graduate
   d. Four-year college graduate
   e. Postgrad student or degree
7. *Current Marital Status*
   a. Single
   b. Married
   c. Widowed
   d. Divorced or separated
8. *Current Rank*
   a. Fire fighter
   b. Paramedic or inspector
   c. Engineer or captain

d. Battalion or division
   chief
e. Assistant or fire
   chief
9. *Religious Background*
   a. Protestant

b. Catholic
c. Other
d. Agnostic or atheist
10. *Father's Occupation*

_____

PART II

1 = SA = Strongly agree
2 = A = Agree
3 = NS = Not sure
4 = D = Disagree
5 = SD = Strongly disagree
   NA = Not applicable

Circle
appropriate
response

	SA	A	NS	D	SD
1. Juveniles who set fires do so as a means of crying for help.	1	2	3	4	5
2. Fire fighters are underpaid.	1	2	3	4	5
3. Kids who set fires are just basically curious.	1	2	3	4	5
4. Kids who set fires are delinquent.	1	2	3	4	5
5. Spouses of fire fighters generally do not understand the demands of their spouse's job.	1	2	3	4	5
6. Arson in America is on the decrease.	1	2	3	4	5
7. Juvenile arson in this country is on the increase.	1	2	3	4	5
8. Fire fighters deal with stress in nonproductive ways.	1	2	3	4	5

9. Fire fighters understand
   kids who set fires more

	SA	A	NS	D	SD	
than the average citizen would.	1	2	3	4	5	
10. Adolescents who get into trouble are more likely to be firesetters.	1	2	3	4	5	
11. Intervention programs for juvenile firesetters are properly a function of the fire department.	1	2	3	4	5	
12. Fire fighters experience less stress than police officers.	1	2	3	4	5	
13. Fire fighters, as compared to non-fire-fighters, have very likely had a history of firesetting.	1	2	3	4	5	
14. My own kids (or younger siblings) have played with fire against my wishes.	1	2	3	4	5	NA
15. Family members of fire fighters are supportive of the fire fighter's profession.	1	2	3	4	5	
16. Fire fighters, in general, enjoy going to fires.	1	2	3	4	5	
17. My own firesetting behavior as a youngster was no different from the average kid's.	1	2	3	4	5	NA
18. Fire fighters are generally extraverted people.	1	2	3	4	5	
19. Fire fighters are overworked in their job.	1	2	3	4	5	
20. Children of fire personnel are less likely to set trouble fires.	1	2	3	4	5	

Appendix B

METHODOLOGY AND TABLES

This appendix explains the methodology used in measuring the behavioral characteristics of sixty-nine firesetters and seventy-eight nonfiresetters.

Between mid-1979 and mid-1983, some sixty-nine firesetters and their parents had completed all three components of the questionnaire (see Appendix A): a detailed parental background questionnaire, a behavioral checklist completed by the parents on their offspring, and a child interview questionnaire.

These sixty-nine completed in-depth questionnaires serve as the data base for our behavioral characteristics study, as discussed in Chapter 3. It should be pointed out that these sixty-nine cases were *not* a random sample of all firesetters apprehended in San Bernardino County during that four-year time period, as not all of the arsonists were assigned to the probation department's Fire Safety and Prevention Program. As we discuss in the body of the book, data were collected on an additional thirty-four cases who had not completed the three sections of the questionnaire. These sixty-nine cases, however, appear to reflect the range and type of firesetters apprehended in this county during the study years. Furthermore, these cases provide us with sufficient numbers to test some of the basic theoretical assumptions that earlier research had formulated and reported on behaviors attributed to juvenile firesetters.

An initial focus of our study was to gather, first, a control group of those juveniles (matched for key background characteristics such as age, race, sex, and family background) and, second, a group of juveniles who had been apprehended by the authorities for offenses other than arson. For each of these two groups, the parents were to be interviewed and were to complete the eighty-four items on the behavior checklist. Obtaining this second offense-sample group proved difficult, and that portion of the project had to be dropped.

The control group sample, however, was obtained. The principal researcher of the project, Dr. Wayne S. Wooden, instructed college students in his criminology classes, as well as behavioral science students in advanced research-methods classes, in the mechanics of administering the questionnaire. See Appendix A for a copy of the control group's questionnaire.

The sample group was gathered by having researchers randomly contact families in the San Bernardino County area that had a child between the ages of four and eighteen. The parent(s) was to complete the questionnaire on the family background and the behavioral characteristics of one of their children. The researchers were also instructed to sample more families with younger male children, from the middle to lower socioeconomic strata. The completed questionnaires were returned anonymously by mail to the principal investigator.

Of the 147 questionnaires administered by students to these randomly selected families, some 83 questionnaires were returned completed (56 percent). Of these, 2 questionnaires were discarded because, in response to one of the questions, the parents indicated that their child had been in trouble with the authorities for having set fires. Because we specifically wanted our control group to be comprised of parents' perceptions of children who had *not* set fires, these two cases were eliminated from the analysis. Further, when running frequency distributions of the two study groups, we noted that we had a higher number number of females, families of Mexican-American background, and families with fewer children in our control group. Because we wished to match our two groups as closely as possible, three (of five) cases were randomly selected out of this subgroup. Thus, we were left with a total of 78 for our control group.

The frequency distributions for both the sixty-nine firesetters and the seventy-eight nonfiresetters are detailed in Table B-1.

Table B-1. Frequency Distributions for Firesetters and Nonfiresetters

	Firesetters (N = 69)	Nonfiresetters (N = 78)
Age categories		
4 to 8	22 (32%)	23 (30%)
9 to 12	23 (34%)	32 (40%)
13 to 17	24 (34%)	23 (30%)
Sex		
Male	61 (88%)	65 (83%)
Female	8 (12%)	13 (17%)
Race		
White	61 (88%)	63 (81%)
Black	3 (5%)	4 (5%)
Mexican-American	5 (7%)	11 (14%)
School		
Elementary	39 (57%)	47 (60%)
Junior high	21 (30%)	22 (28%)
High school	9 (13%)	9 (12%)
Family		
Natural child	53 (77%)	74 (95%)
Adopted	9 (13%)	3 (4%)
Foster/stepchild	4 (6%)	0 (0%)
Not reported	3 (4%)	1 (1%)

Table B-2. Stealing among Firesetters versus Nonfiresetters[a]

| Group | Stealing | | | Row total |
	Never	Sometimes	Frequently	
Nonfiresetters	68	10	0	78
	65%	28%	0	53%
Firesetters	37	26	6	69
	35%	72%	100%	47%
Column total	105	36	6	147

[a] $\chi^2(2) = 21.79417$, $p \leq .0001$

Table B-3. Truancy among Firesetters versus Nonfiresetters[a]

| Group | Truancy | | | Row total |
	Never	Sometimes	Frequently	
Nonfiresetters	73	5	0	78
	64%	20%	0%	54%
Firesetters	42	20	5	67
	36%	80%	100%	46%
Column total	115	25	5	145

[a] $\chi^2(2) = 21.64662$, $p \leq .0001$

Table B-4. School Problems among Firesetters versus Nonfiresetters[a]

| Group | Behavior problems in school | | | Row total |
	Never	Sometimes	Frequently	
Nonfiresetters	42	30	5	77
	67%	48%	26%	53%
	55%	39%	6%	
Firesetters	21	33	14	68
	33%	52%	74%	47%
	30%	49%	21%	
Column total	63	63	19	145

[a] $\chi^2(2) = 10.88935$, $p \leq .004$

Table B-5. Learning Problems among Firesetters versus Nonfiresetters[a]

	Learning problems in school			Row total
Group	Never	Sometimes	Frequently	
Nonfiresetters	43	31	4	78
	61%	55%	20%	53%
	55%	45%	5%	
Firesetters	28	25	16	69
	39%	45%	80%	47%
	41%	36%	23%	
Column total	71	56	20	147

[a] $\chi^2(2) = 10.50021, p \leq .005$

Table B-6. Easily Led by Peers among Firesetters versus Nonfiresetters[a]

	Easily led by peers			Row total
Group	Never	Sometimes	Frequently	
Nonfiresetters	17	53	5	75
	53%	63%	18%	52%
Firesetters	15	31	22	68
	47%	37%	82%	48%
Column total	32	84	27	143

[a] $\chi^2(2) = 16.28698, p \leq .0003$

Table B-7. History of Behavioral Problems among Firesetters versus Nonfiresetters[a]

Group	History of behavioral problems			Row total
	Never	Sometimes	Frequently	
Nonfiresetters	66	7	1	74
	61%	32%	9%	52%
Firesetters	43	15	10	68
	39%	68%	91%	48%
Column total	109	22	11	142

[a] $\chi^2(2) = 14.89902$, $p \leq .0006$

Table B-8. Plays Alone among Firesetters versus Nonfiresetters[a]

Group	Plays alone			Row total
	Never	Sometimes	Frequently	
Nonfiresetters	18	59	0	77
	44%	62%	0%	53%
Firesetters	23	36	8	67
	56%	38%	100%	47%
Column total	41	95	8	144

[a] $\chi^2(2) = 13.54907$, $p \leq .001$

Table B-9. Hyperactivity among Firesetters versus Nonfiresetters[a]

Group	Hyperactivity			Row total
	Never	Sometimes	Frequently	
Nonfiresetters	33	36	7	76
	52%	63%	29%	52%
Firesetters	31	21	17	69
	48%	37%	71%	48%
Column total	64	57	24	145

[a] $\chi^2(2) = 7.85692$, $p \leq .02$

Table B-10. Cruelty to Animals by Age of Firesetters[a]

| | Cruelty to animals | | | Row |
Age of firesetters	Never	Sometimes	Frequently	total
4 to 8	12 54%	7 32%	3 14%	22 32%
9 to 12	21 91%	2 9%	0 0%	23 33%
13 to 17	21 88%	2 8%	1 4%	24 35%
Column total	54 78%	11 16%	4 6%	69

[a] $\chi^2(4) = 11.22581$, $p \le .02$

Table B-11. Bedwetting (after Age Three) by Age of Firesetters[a]

| | Bedwetting (after age 3) | | | Row |
Age of firesetters	Never	Sometimes	Frequently	total
4 to 8	13 59%	5 23%	4 18%	22 32%
9 to 12	13 56%	8 35%	2 9%	23 34%
13 to 17	21 92%	1 4%	1 4%	23 34%
Column total	47	14	7	68

[a] $\chi^2(4) = 9.90892$, $p \le .04$

Table B-12. Summary Table of Significant Behavior Characteristics
and Levels of Significance for Each Age Group of Firesetters

Behavior	4–8	9–12	13–17
Hyperactivity	.003		
Lack of concentration			
Learning problems (home or school)		.05	
Behavior problems in school			.0005
Impulsive (acts before he or she thinks)			.05
Impatient	.001		.001
Accidents		.03	.005
Convulsions or "spells"			
Wets during day			
Extreme mood swings	.007		
Need for security	.05		.007
Need for affection			.02
Depression		.04	
Unusual movements—tics			.04
Stuttering		.02	
Bedwetting (after age three)			
Soiling (after age three)			
Lying	.002	.03	
Excessive and uncontrolled anger	.04	.008	.01
Violence		.03	.009
Stealing	.02	.0000	.01
Truancy			.03
Cruelty to animals			.002
Cruelty to children		.003	
Fighting with peers		.008	.007
Fighting with siblings			.04
Destroys toys of others			
Destroys own toys	.05	.02	
Runs away from home or school		.02	.006
Disobeys	.006		.02
Long history of severe behavioral difficulties	.004		.0003
Child is a poor loser			.0008
Child expresses anger by hurting other's things			

(Continued)

Table B-12. (Continued)

Behavior	4–8	9–12	13–17
Child expresses anger by hurting self or something he or she likes	.05		
Child has been in trouble with police			.007
Easily led by peers		.04	
Jealousy			.001
Temper tantrums			.05
Doesn't play with other children			.03
Shows off			
Severe depressions or withdrawal			.002
Child is good in sports			
Shyness			.007
Extreme goodness			
Sexual activity with others			
Stomachaches		.05	
Nightmares			
Other sleep or waking problems		.0008	.03
Anxiety		.03	.01
Fantasizing			.03
Poor or no eye contact			.01
Child has twitches (eyes, face, etc.)			.006
Crying			.05
Nail biting			
Vomiting			.004
Thumb sucking			
Aches and pains			.007
Chewing odd things			
Constipation			.01
Diarrhea			
Masturbation			
Curiosity about fire			
Plays with fire	.04	.006	
Panicked when fire got out of control	.006		
Fires set some distance from child's home			
Child proud or boastful regarding her or his fire setting		.01	

(Continued)

Table B-12. (Continued)

Behavior	4–8	9–12	13–17
Stares at fires for long periods of time		.05	.04
Daydreams or talks about fire			
Unusual look on child's face as he or she frequently stares at fires			
Family discord			
Father or mother absent			
Family has moved with child			
Child has seen a therapist			.001
Other family member has seen a therapist	.05	.03	
Parent has serious health problem			.003
Marriage is unhappy	.04		.01
Mother's discipline is ineffective			
Father's discipline is ineffective			
Unusual fantasies			.05
Strange thought patterns			.001
Speech, bizarre, illogical, or irrational		.002	
Out of touch with reality		.02	.0003
Strange quality about child			.006
Self-imposed diets			.04
Sleepwalking			
Phobias			.002
Fears			.05
Child plays alone		.006	
Total	15	23	44

Table B-13. Easily Led by Peers for Preteenage Group by Severity
Level[a]

| Severity level | Easily led by peers | | | Row total |
	Never	Sometimes	Frequently	
Minor concern	3	5	0	8
	75%	50%	0%	35%
Moderate concern	0	4	6	10
	0%	40%	67%	43%
Major concern	1	1	3	5
	25%	10%	33%	22%
Column total	4	10	9	23

[a] $\chi^2(4) = 9.74625, p \le .04$

Table B-14. Strange Thought Patterns for Teenage Group by Severity
Level[a]

| Severity level | Strange thought patterns | | | Row total |
	Never	Sometimes	Frequently	
Minor concern	8	1	0	9
	44%	25%	0%	39%
Moderate concern	10	0	0	10
	56%	0%	0%	44%
Major concern	0	3	1	4
	0%	75%	100%	17%
Column total	18	4	1	23

[a] $\chi^2(4) = 18.19059, p \le .001$

Table B-15. Jealousy for Teenage Group by Severity Level[a]

	Jealousy			Row
Severity level	Never	Sometimes	Frequently	total
Minor concern	7	2	0	9
	50%	29%	0%	37%
Moderate concern	7	4	0	11
	50%	57%	0%	46%
Major concern	0	1	3	4
	0%	14%	100%	17%
Column total	14	7	3	24

[a] $\chi^2(4) = 18.33766$, $p \leq .001$

Table B-16. Type of School-Related Fires by Sex[a]

	Sex		Row
Type	Male	Female	total
"Playing with matches"	108	17	125
	22%	35%	23%
Fireworks	238	9	247
	49%	19%	46%
Off-campus fires	142	22	164
	29%	46%	31%
Column total	488	48	536
	91%	9%	

[a] $\chi^2(2) = 15.85435$, $p \leq .0004$

Table B-17. Type of School-Related Fires by Age[a]

Age	Type of fire			Row total
	"Playing with matches"	Fireworks	Off-campus fires	
3 to 8	34	1	44	79
	27%	1%	27%	15%
9 to 11	14	4	41	59
	11%	2%	25%	11%
12 to 13	33	67	23	123
	26%	27%	14%	23%
14 to 15	33	117	30	180
	26%	47%	18%	33%
16 to 18	11	58	26	95
	9%	23%	16%	18%
Column total	125	247	164	536
	23%	46%	31%	

[a] $\chi^2(8) = 158.91348$, $p \leq .0001$

Table B-18. Commitment Offense of First Commitments to the Youth
Authority, 1971, 1976, and 1981[a]

| | 1971 | | 1976 | | 1981 | |
Offense	No.	%	No.	%	No.	%
Total, all offenses	3,218	100.0	3,559	100.0	4,083	100.0
Offenses against persons	839	26.1	1,577	44.3	2,004	49.1
Homicide	73	2.3	158	4.4	210	5.1
Robbery	427	13.3	876	24.6	1,008	24.7
Assault and battery	274	8.5	442	12.4	603	14.8
Rape (violent)	51	1.6	83	2.4	140	3.4
Kidnapping	14	0.4	18	0.5	43	1.1
Offenses against property	1,122	34.9	1,503	42.2	1,833	44.9
Burglary	533	16.6	912	25.6	1,134	27.8
Theft (except auto)	252	7.8	295	8.3	371	9.1
Auto theft	247	7.7	231	6.5	259	6.3
Forgery and checks	66	2.1	36	1.0	25	0.6
Arson	*24*	*0.7*	*29*	*0.8*	*44*	*1.1*
Narcotics and drugs	605	18.8	125	3.5	86	2.1
All other offenses	652	20.2	354	10.0	160	3.9

[a] From the *1981 Annual Report* of the Department of the Youth Authority, State of California, Sacramento, California, p. 23. Reprinted by permission.

Table B-19. Personality Diagnosis of Youth Authority Firesetters by
Race[a]

| Personality diagnosis | Race | | | Row total |
	White	Hispanic	Black	
Unsocialized	10	4	1	15
	11%	14%	6%	11%
Conformist	31	19	14	64
	35%	65%	78%	47%
Neurotic	47	6	3	56
	53%	21%	16%	42%
Column total	88	29	18	135
	65%	22%	13%	

[a] $\chi^2(4) = 17.66733$, $p \leq .001$, missing observations = 57

Table B-20. Fire Fighters Study

	% Agree	% Not sure	% Disagree
Attitudes toward juveniles who set fires			
Juveniles who set fires do so as a means of crying for help.	47%	24%	29%
Kids who set fires are just basically curious.	46	21	33
Kids who set fires are delinquents.	21	31	48
Adolescents who get into trouble are more likely to be firesetters.	29	32	39
Fire fighters and their job			
Fire fighters are underpaid.	86	5	9
Fire fighters are overworked in their job.	18	18	64
Fire fighters experience less stress than police officers.	20	15	65
Fire fighters deal with stress in nonproductive ways.	45	21	34
Fire fighters, in general, enjoy going to fires.	85	9	6
Spouses of fire fighters generally do not understand the demands of their spouse's job.	46	10	44
Family members of fire fighters are supportive of the fire fighter's profession.	93	5	2
Fire fighters are generally extraverted people.	59	20	21
Fire fighters understand kids who set fires more than the average citizen would.	45	26	29

(Continued)

Table B-20. (Continued)

	% Agree	% Not sure	% Disagree
Fire fighters attitudes toward arson			
Arson in America is on the decrease.	9%	10%	81%
Juvenile arson in this country is on the increase.	62	30	8
Intervention programs for juvenile firesetters are properly a function of the fire department.	60	21	19
The firesetting behavior of fire fighters			
Fire fighters, as compared to nonfirefighters, have very likely had a history of firesetting.	9	19	72
My own firesetting behavior as a youngster was no different from the average kid's.[a]	55	18	9
Children of fire personnel are less likely to set trouble fires.	51	27	23
My own kids (or younger siblings) have played with fire against my wishes.[b]	15	14	35

[a] 18% responded to this question by answering "not applicable."
[b] 36% responded to this question by answering "not applicable."

Table B-21. Fire Fighters' Self-Reported Fire Activity by Offspring's
Fire Activity[a]

My own kids (or younger siblings) have played with fire against my wishes.	My own firesetting behavior as a youngster was no different from the average kid's.			Row total
	Agree	Not sure	Disagree	
Agree	13	5	1	19
	19%	23%	3%	15%
Not sure	11	3	1	15
	16%	14%	3%	12%
Disagree	44	14	31	89
	65%	63%	94%	72%
Column total	68	22	33	123
	55%	18%	27%	

[a] $\chi^2(4) = 10.74157$, $p \leq .03$, missing observations = 5

Appendix C

"LEARN NOT TO BURN" KNOWLEDGE TEST

Please mark the correct answer on your answer sheet:

1. (*Example*) Very young children should:
   A. learn how to light a fire with matches
   B. never use matches
   C. use matches only when older children are with them
   D. have a bucket of water nearby when they are lighting fires
2. When a home fire occurs, it is most important that you:
   A. try to put the fire out
   B. call the fire department
   C. get out first and then call the fire department
   D. close all the windows
3. If you cannot get indoors during a storm with lightning, you should:
   A. stand beneath the nearest tree
   B. get to the highest point in the area
   C. lie down in the lowest point in the area
   D. seek shelter in the nearest car
4. If there is a fire in an oven, the best thing to do is:
   A. turn off heat and leave oven door closed
   B. turn off heat and open the oven door
   C. throw water on the fire
   D. take the burning food out of the oven

5. If there is a fire in the home, you should:
   A. hurry out of the building taking nothing
   B. take only the possessions that can be easily taken
   C. take only your valuable possessions
   D. stop long enough to get your pets
6. Gasoline should never be used to clean greasy car parts because:
   A. its odor is strong
   B. it is not a good cleaner
   C. vapors may ignite when they come in contact with ignition sources like lighted cigarettes
   D. it may remove the finish on the parts
7. How should you keep your tent lighted when camping?
   A. a campfire small enough not to set the tent on fire
   B. candles
   C. a flashlight
   D. matches
8. For your family's safety it is most important that you:
   A. have a fire extinguisher
   B. have fire insurance
   C. know the phone number of the Fire Department
   D. have a home fire escape plan and a smoke detector
9. If your clothes catch on fire, you should:
   A. run to put out the flames.
   B. drop to the ground and roll.
   C. get water to throw on the flames.
   D. take off the burning clothes.
10. If a skillet catches on fire, the best thing to do is:
    A. turn off the fire, cover the skillet to put it out
    B. quickly and carefully carry the skillet outside
    C. immediately call the Fire Department
    D. go out to eat
11. Smoke detectors should be placed:
    A. in the kitchen next to the stove
    B. in the attic
    C. outside the bedroom areas
    D. in the garage just above the combustible materials

12. The most important part of a home fire safety plan is to have:
    A. the electricity turned off
    B. the Fire Department's phone number handy
    C. alternate escape routes and a meeting place outside
    D. fire extinguishers
13. When cooking at a stove, it is most important that you should wear:
    A. clothes that fit loosely around arms and body
    B. clothes that fit closely around arms and body
    C. nylon clothing
    D. cotton clothing
14. When you are in a smoke-filled house, you should:
    A. keep your head up and call for help
    B. hold your breath and run out of the smoke
    C. keep your eyes closed and walk out of the smoke
    D. crawl low out of the smoke
15. Which one of the following fabrics is most difficult to ignite and burn?
    A. cotton
    B. synthetics
    C. silk
    D. wool
16. The type of heater that does not need a way to allow fumes to escape is:
    A. coal
    B. wood
    C. electric
    D. portable gas or oil
17. Gasoline should be stored:
    A. in the trunk of the car
    B. in large glass jars in the garage
    C. in a locked closet
    D. in a special safety can outside the house
18. Instead of using an electrical cord having exposed or frayed wires you should:
    A. replace the entire cord

B. tape the exposed part of the wire

C. replace the exposed part of the wire

D. cover exposed part of the wire with a carpet

19. If you have more appliances than you have electrical outlets, you should:

A. put three-way plugs into the outlet

B. use extension cords

C. use only grounded plugs

D. plug in only one or two appliances at a time.

20. If a person with burns appears to be in a state of shock, you should:

A. walk the person to keep him awake

B. have him lie down and cover him with a blanket

C. give him artificial respiration

D. put a cool cloth on his forehead

21. Which one of the following is not needed for a fire to occur?

A. fuel

B. heat

C. nitrogen

D. oxygen

22. For minor burns you should:

A. put cool water on the burn

B. put an oily or greasy substance on the burn

C. bandage the burn tightly

D. wash the burn with soap and warm water

23. Smoke contains:

A. carbon monoxide

B. ammonia

C. methane

D. peroxide

24. Which one of the following is considered most flammable or combustible?

A. kerosene

B. gasoline

C. lighter fluid

D. paint thinner

25. If you are walking along the street and see smoke coming out of a building, you should:
   A. do nothing because someone may have already reported it
   B. wait to see if the smoke becomes a big fire
   C. call the fire department immediately
   D. go into the building to warn the people

Answers

1. B	6. C	11. C	16. C	21. C
2. C	7. C	12. C	17. D	22. A
3. C	8. D	13. B	18. A	23. A
4. A	9. B	14. D	19. D	24. B
5. A	10. A	15. D	20. B	25. C

INDEX

259

Family (*cont.*)
  playing-with-fire firesetters, 46
  psychological profile classification
    and, 125, 126, 127
  severely disturbed firesetters, 89–
    90
  typical male offenders, 119
Fathers. *See also* Family; Mothers;
    Parents
  crying-for-help firesetters, 54, 57
  delinquent firesetters, 72
  female firesetters, 97–98, 102–103
  severely disturbed firesetters, 84
  sexual abuse by, 99
Federal Bureau of Investigation
    (FBI), 7, 9, 10, 18, 168
Female firesetters, 94–100, 110
  case examples of, 97–98
  motivation and, 96
  peer groups and, 95–96
  sexual abuse of, 98–100
  sexual activity and, 102–103
  typical profile of, 119–120
Fineman, Kenneth R., 51, 187–189
Fire(s)
  fascination of, 10–11
  indifference to, 197
  mythology and, 11–12
  religion and, 11–12
  society and, 16
  symbolism of, 130
Fire "buffs," 137–138
Fire departments, 24. *See also* Fire
    fighters
  counseling by, 140
  fire-education programs, 139,
    198, 199
  fires and, 146
  firesetters in, 5
  habits of personnel in, 144
  job satisfaction in, 145, 146
  motivational assessment of, 143–
    144
  playing-with-fire firesetters, 43
  questionnaire for, 141–143

Fire departments (*cont.*)
  stress and, 145–146, 147
  treatment and, 179
Fire-education programs, 139, 198,
    199
Fire fighters, 135–163
  arson by, 135–137
  arson rates and, 148–149
  children of, 151–152
  families of, 146–147, 153
  firesetters and, 17–18, 72, 137
  firesetting history of, 149–150
  health of, 147
  image of, 198
  interview with, 153–163
  personal habits of, 144
  personality of, 147–148
  questionnaire form for, 231–234
  sexuality and, 14, 96–97
  summary table of, 249–251
  treatment of arsonists and, 185–
    186
Firehawk program, 185–186, 199
Fireplaces, 16–17
Fire prevention
  delinquent firesetters, 64–65
  fire departments, 139, 140
  fire-safety education, 197–199
  firesetter assistance, 202–203
Fire Prevention Week, 199–202
Fire-safety education
  adults, 199–200
  community programs, 199
  prevention and, 197
  schools, 198–199
Fire-safety precautions, 181–182
Fire-safety programs, 179, 180
Firesetters. *See also* Crying-for-help
    firesetters; Delinquent
    firesetters; Playing-with-fire
    firesetters; Severely disturbed
    firesetters
  academic performance and, 31,
    32
  assistance for, 202–203